Tactical Handgun 1

Instructor Zulu

This Manual Contains Graphic Images & Topics

Table of Contents

Course Objectives..p. 6

ZuluSafe Briefing..p. 7

Introduction..p. 9

Chapter 1: Training For Tomorrow...p. 12

Chapter 2: So What Is Force Science?......................................p. 21

Chapter 3: The Law..p. 33

Chapter 4: Concealed Carry...p. 43

Chapter 5: Zulu's Top Picks...p. 53

Chapter 6: Handgun Safety..p. 72

Chapter 7: Loading & Reloading...p. 84

Chapter 8: Malfunction Mitigation..p. 90

Chapter 9: Basic Marksmanship...p. 100

Chapter 10: Situational Awareness & Threat ID........................p. 106

Chapter 11: Multi-Threat Engagement....................................p. 110

Chapter 12: Defensive Shooting..p. 116

Practical Exercises..p. 127

Course Objectives

1. Understand how to train for a gunfight.
2. Learn about ZuluFight Dry-Fire Training System.
3. Understand Force Science and the dynamics of Firearms Self-Defense.
4. Understand Self-Defense Laws.
5. Learn about ZuluShield and a Preemptive Firearms Legal Defense.
6. Understand Concealed Carry.
7. Understand which firearms are best suited for a gunfight.
8. Understand which ammunition is best suited for a gunfight.
9. Understand which holsters are best for what.
10. Understand Handgun Safety.
11. Understand Firearms Security.
12. Understand Loading & Reloading.
13. Understand Malfunction Mitigation.
14. Understand Basic Marksmanship.
15. Understand Situational Awareness & Threat ID.
16. Learn about ABCs Tactical Awareness Aides.
17. Understand Multi-Threat Engagement.
18. Understand Defensive Shooting.

ZuluSafe Briefing

Tactical Handgun 1 Safety Rules:

Upon arrival at the range, all firearms shall be inspected by the Range Master or Range Safety Officer(s) prior to any handling of any weapons whatsoever. Pay careful attention to the Range Master and Safety Officer(s) at all times. Pay special attention to how you handle firearms throughout the entirety of the class, to include Dry-Fire training firearms. Maintain situational awareness at all times.

ZuluSafe Cardinal Safety Rules:

1. Treat ALL firearms as if they are ALWAYS loaded.
2. Keep your fingers OFF the trigger and OUTSIDE the trigger-guard until you are justified and ready to shoot.
3. NEVER point your muzzle at anything or anyone you're not justified and willing to kill.
4. Be SURE of your Threat and what stands beyond.

ZuluSafe Range Rules:

1. We operate a 'Hot Range' meaning firearms are treated as if they are loaded at all times. Handguns shall remain holstered and long-guns slung and oriented so they are pointed down towards the ground at all times, unless otherwise instructed by the Range Master or Range Safety Officer(s).
2. All loading and unloading of firearms shall be conducting ONLY at the firing line, while under direct supervision of the Range Master or Range Safety Officer(s).
3. While re-loading and unloading firearms magazines, you will assure your handgun remains holstered and your long-gun is slung and oriented so that it points down towards the ground at ALL times.
4. All range firing shall be conducted under the direct supervision of the Range Master or Range Safety Officer(s).
5. When actively engaged in a course of fire, KEEP FIREARMS POINTED DOWN RANGE AT ALL TIMES. This course involves movement exercises and courses of fire, which

place you in close and dangerous proximity to other students and staff. You shall maintain situational awareness at all times and assure you NEVER point your firearm at other students or staff members.

6. NEVER move forward of the firing line until cleared and directed to do so by the Range Master or Range Safety Officer(s). This includes the retrieval of items dropped on the deck.

7. Call out loudly if you do not understand a command. When in doubt <u>DON'T SHOOT</u>!

8. If you notice an unsafe or hazardous situation loudly yell "<u>CEASEFIRE</u>!" If a Ceasefire order is given, immediately STOP and freeze. If holding a firearm, place your trigger finger off the trigger and outside the trigger guard. Wait for further direction from the Range Master and Range Safety Officer(s).

9. Eye and hearing protection is required at all times. Due to lead exposure, wash your hands prior to eating or drinking.

Lead Exposure Risk:

Firearms training poses obvious risks of lead exposure. It is imperative that you take appropriate action to mitigate these risks, by thoroughly washing your hands with soap and water, prior to eating, drinking or smoking.

Assumption of Responsibility:

Firearms training poses obvious risks of serious physical injury or death. There is also an increased risk of lead exposure and hearing loss. Maintain situational awareness at all times throughout this training. Your firearm can only discharge if it is loaded and the trigger is depressed. Regardless of where your firearm is pointed, it will fire. You are solely and legally responsible for your actions before, during and following this training. Pay attention and maintain safety at ALL times.

Introduction

Today the firearm has become one of the most controversially misunderstood manmade objects in existence. In fact, there isn't another form of apparatus on Earth which has caused as much a stir in all of creation than that of the firearm. While it is loved my many, it is utterly loathed by a multitude more. Regardless of one's personal views and beliefs, there is no better device capable of offering the practical effectiveness which a firearm affords in a deadly encounter with another human being. There is simply no better way of overcoming a threat than through the effective application of fire.

There are a multitude of reasons why individuals choose to possess firearms. To some possession is a sort of right-of-passage, a way of showing one's solidarity to the concept of being 'Free'. It's as if possessing a firearm, in some way proves their patriotism and commitment to 'The Cause'. Most owners share in an almost euphoric feeling of power that is easily perceived as a sort of fanatical obsession by objectors. Some possess them because they simply like having them around. They hoard them as collector's pieces for show-and-tell. Others enjoy shooting them for competition and recreation. Many have them for hunting and sport. Still others retain them for defensive purposes, as a means of securing one's life as a last resort.

While there are slew of reasons for why firearms remain an important and unmistaken reality of our daily lives, their conception and the mere fact of their existence is for one reason and one reason only, to kill. The firearm was designed as a means of providing a soldier a better, more efficient way of destroying their enemy from a much greater distance and in greater number than through the use of the sword. Since its conception in China in the 10th Century, the firearm has played a pivotal role in the theater of conflict and has extended and sustained the existence of life in every corner of the World.

Firearms don't have super powers; they're not a form of magical bad-guy kryptonite, capable of magically overpowering your adversary through proximity alone. Simply possessing a firearm is useless. In an untrained hand the firearm is dangerous and completely incapable, a worthlessly expensive paperweight. However, in the hands of a master, the firearm is a tool capable of thwarting even the most unexpected and well planned attack.

Successfully surviving armed conflict requires an abundance of knowledge and skill. You may be able to touch rounds at 25 yards with a handgun. You may even be a champion competitor with a shelf full of trophies and ribbons. However, utilizing a firearm in conflict is the most stressfully fluid and dynamic task known to man. Relying on 'Preconceived' ideas of make-believe, founded on 'Assumptions' derived from Hollywood action films and depending on your perceived abilities on a range or at a match, may just prove to cause your demise.

To the surprise of many, recently released FBI statistics show a consentient downward trend in overall crime. While on one hand this could appear to be an amazing blessing, the reality though, speaks to something vastly different. Hidden beneath the surface of statistical data, and cloaked in politically motivated double-talk, lies a latent cancer called 'Statistical Aggregation.' FBI crime statistics are comprised of two main categories, 'Property Crimes' and 'Violent Crimes'. Each category is aggregated and made-up of a group of individually composed and distinctly different kinds of crimes. Each category ranges from extremely petty to extraordinarily vicious.

The problem arises when one looks closely at what the FBI is attempting to communicate. Their intent is to convince citizens that we live in a much safer world than 5 years ago, knowing full and well extremely violent forms of 'Random Crime' has skyrocketed since 2009. How so? When focusing on 'Violent Crime' you will find that this category represents assault, robbery, rape and murder. Simple right? It is until you introduce the notion 'Random Occurrence'. While typical murder; amongst individuals who know each other, has dramatically dropped, random acts of murder have starkly risen. When considering random acts of violent assault, you'll also find a consistent upward trend. The same is true for rape and aggravated robberies. So while 95% of typical violent crime has dropped, 5% of the most dangerous acts of violence have skyrocketed.

It's this 5% which represents 'Random Crime' against random citizens, in random communities, that should be of the greatest concern to you. When also considering these acts of random violence are no longer isolated to America's inter-city ghettos, you quickly realize that nobody is truly safe. When you remove the rose filtered lenses the FBI fools you into using. When you step back and see crime for what it truly is, it's then that you realize just how vulnerable you actually are. By actively looking deeper into the truth of the matter, it's only then that you can begin to see what they're attempting to hide. While the FBI says 'Crime' has dropped, a growing number of Sheriffs and Police Chiefs across our country are saying something completely different. In fact, they're advising citizens to arm themselves and be prepared to defend their lives and NOT to rely on local Law Enforcement services to save them. This represents a startling shift in Public Safety and should be of grave concern and a major wake-up call to you.

The truth? Everyday random acts of the most extreme violence are occurring across America. From the inter-city of Chicago's West Side, to the sleepy town of Oak Hill North Carolina, random citizens are being slaughtered at an alarming rate. Across our otherwise 'Safe' country, a growing number of Home Invasions, Active Shooter/Active Threat Incidents, random and horribly violent rapes and demonically gruesome acts of murder, are growing at an exponential rate. As if it couldn't be worse, violent attacks against Law Enforcement have also starkly risen.

The reality is that recent FBI crime statistics show that 'Crime' has made a polar shift. Prior to 2009 petty crimes; to include white collar embezzlement and low level theft and car break-ins, have dramatically decreased. This suggests that the 'Everyday

Citizen' has found a more ethical way of living. Yet due to budget cuts since 2009, prisons, jails and mental health facilities across America have been flooding our communities with viciously violent offenders at a greater rate than ever before. We experienced a similar occurrence in the early 80's and think to yourselves about just how violent the 1990's was. Now multiply that exponentially and you'll understand why police agencies are urging the public to arm themselves. It's the mere fact that these individuals' psychotic episodes are going completely un-checked, which posse such a great risk to the average everyday random citizen. It's this growing number of schizophrenic sociopaths who have caused our polar crime shift to go from white collar to completely demonic. While the everyday citizen has found a way of being better mannered, the influx of completely insane and violently pervasive predators have perfected the 'Craft' of identifying societies' weaknesses so as to capitalize on our most vulnerable, while bringing terror to even the sleepiest community.

The answer? I mentioned it above. From Michigan to Florida, Indiana to Oregon, Law Enforcing officials are encouraging their citizens to arm themselves and NOT to rely on 911. But is it really that simple? Will simply arming yourself protect you against random acts of violence? Not without proper study and training.

Tactical Handgun 1 (TH1) introduces you to the concepts related to the subject of Firearms Self-Defense. Defending one's self with a firearm is an extraordinarily arduous task, extremely dangerous and requires great skill and knowledge. Effectively wining a gun battle is much more than simply being a good shot on the range. The subject of Firearms Self-Defense is serious, it's not a Hollywood action movie or a first person video game. There's no re-spawning in a real-world gun fight. The consequences and outcomes are real and will determine if you live or if you die.

The theories and objectives communicated throughout this course are intended to provide you with the building blocks of a Tactical Squared Response to a deadly encounter. Winning a gunfight is not about learning to consistently shoot bull's-eyes, nor does it have anything to do with achieving top scores at a 3 Gun or IPSC match. IHD is about learning the art of playing Tactical Chess while your opponent is left playing Checkers. It's about wining gunfights. It's about learning to kill your advisory before he kills you. This course has one overriding objective. The goal is to provide you with proven foundational combatives. IHD will facilitate the development of the necessary skills required and teach you how to use your firearm as it was intended. IHD is your first step on your path to firearms mastery. Learn the art of Firearms Self-Defense so you can quickly and effectively defeat a threat to your mortal existence with confidence and competence.

This course affords a better grasp of the real-world dynamics of conflict and how it relates to the application of defensive firearms use. IHD will equip you with a much deeper understanding of the realities of armed defense while also installing the highest possible degree of firearms safety, proficiency and confidence, while also introducing you to extremely practical, effective and proven tactics capable of overcoming future deadly attack.

Zulu Tactical offers a plethora of firearms training opportunities from basic to extremely advanced. IHD is your first step along this journey to firearms mastery. Tomorrow's deadly attack is overcome before you even meet your adversary. Take advantage of all our courses and discover the secrets of Tactical Chess. Rely on wisdom and skill as opposed to assumption. Train Today So You're Ready Tomorrow!

1
Training For Tomorrow

In discussing the topic of Firearms Self-Defense, most people unintentionally focus on only one aspect, the 'Purchase' of a firearm. Unfortunately, the vast majority of armed citizens completely ignore three other equally important elements:

1. Without sound combatives training, your fancy new firearm is useless and in all reality it places you and others at greater risk.

2. Without sound understanding of the laws associated with Self-Defense, there's no way for you to develop a decision making process, which provides reasonable responses to perceived threats.

3. Without a sound Legal Defense plan, should you be forced to actually use Deadly Force in defense of your life or someone else's, your entire Legal Defense strategy will be based on 'Chance'.

The intent of this chapter is to point-out (3) important elements to 'Sound Combatives Training':

1. Firearms Kata
2. Stress Inoculation
3. Tactical Training

Your Self-Defense Response to tomorrow's deadly threat is determined by what you do today, to assure it's the 'Best' response capable of overcoming even the most extreme circumstances tomorrow. Determining what response is 'Best' and what method of training has the greatest potential to condition the 'Right' response, is the most essential decision you'll make.

Today there is a smorgasbord of training systems and methodologies. Sadly, that's how most people approach the concept of 'Firearms Training', as though it were a meal or a means of filling one's appetite. Other's approach it from a most passive perspective of simply learning to shoot accurately or draw quickly and completely overlook the 'Fight' in tomorrow's Fight. You see most people fail to realize just how significate this type of training actually is because they don't take the time to first process and digest exactly 'What' they're training for. When it comes to Firearms Self-Defense, the reality is that said 'Training' is supposed to give you the ability to provide a perfect response to a completely random, surprised attack on your actual existence. The gravity of such an attack is such that your 'Response' is your ONLY hope for survival. So selection of the 'Right' training method boils down to determining how much your 'Life' means to you.

When it relates to Firearms Self-Defense, the word 'Training' is often where people get tripped up. Since its use is so common, embodying all forms of instruction and schooling, from everyday academics to sports and even vocational, the concept of 'Training' is easily misunderstood when it comes to Self-Defense. When it relates to Self-Defense, it's meaning has a depth and density, which simply can't be compared to any other form.

As was just stated, training for tomorrow's battle means your attempting to develop a physical response to a completely unknown future circumstance, that poses an immediate threat to your actual existence. What this means is that you must develop a 'Perfect' response to a completely unknown situation, where 'Second Place' means you lose and loosing means you die.

Other forms of training such as academics, sports or vocational type instruction, all allow for a particular degree of error. For instance, academically the standard is a (C), as long as you maintain that average, you pass. Obviously a (B) or (A) would result in a much more competitive outcome, giving you higher placement amongst your peer-group. However, when it relates to an actual fight for your life, your level of proficiency MUST translate to 'Straight A's' and when the test comes, the ONLY acceptable outcome is an (A+). If you do not meet that standard, the only probable outcome is death. It's really that simple. Are there people who survive battles with no preparation at all? Yes. However, theirs is all based on 'Chance'. Ask yourself this, would you bet your life on a game of Craps, would you wager it all away on one roll of the dice? If your answer was yes, this training's not for you. However, if your answer was like the vast majority of other reasonably minded individuals, then this chapter should be studied and re-studied, so you arrive at the 'Right' decision.

Firearms Kata...

Your first step towards developing a squared away Self-Defense Response, begins with understanding the composition of Firearms Self-Defense as a whole. Once you've fully grasped the realization, that the act of 'Using' a firearm to defend oneself, requires both a Physical and Psychological process, then you're able to go about honing each aspect with intelligence and an acute attention to detail.

Let's dissect the 'Physical' component or the 'Kinesis' of firearms. Of course, what we all hope for is to somehow acquire an instantaneous response or 'Reflex' to an immediate and deadly threat. Much like the 'Patellar Reflex Test' your doctor does when they tap your knee with that rubber mallet, we hope to develop a defense mechanism that fires immediately upon first contact and hits the mark accurately and without error. Now we all know that nobody is born a fighter or an expert shot, all that is acquired through training. So the obvious question is, which training method is best? When it relates to the kinesis of shooting; the culmination of isolated movements for one overall response, there are a plethora of methods available.

Unfortunately, the vast majority of firearms training methods prove to be counterproductive and in many cases actually place the trainee in a much more compromised position than if they wouldn't have even trained at all. It's been said that "Practice Makes Perfect" so many are fooled into believing that if something looks good on paper or the masses support it, then it's got to be worth their time and money. Well, I'd wager that 'Poor Practice' is the fastest way to learn how to lose and in this arena, losing gets you dead. Instead of conditioning appropriate responses, most training methods place the trainee at a disadvantage, where they wind-up wasting time, money and effort, all while conditioning responses, which not only attempt to violate the Laws of Physics, but rely on concepts and movements which are completely impossible to reproduce during an actual real-life fight.

Have you ever wondered how Michael Jordan became the super star he was and still is? During an interview, Jordan claimed that the only way he became so good at his craft, was because his mother made him shoot 'Free Throws' every day as child for hours at a time. This concept; 'Free Throws' and its relationship with Firearms Self-Defense is vitally important to grasp.

A Free Throw costs nothing and is a 'Free' attempt at an easy point. As an added bonus, all 'Time' stops and everyone waits for the shooter to concentrate and take his time for two perfect shots. In the NBA, most games often rely on a team's ability to sink these all important 'Free' shots. In any given game you'll see dozens of attempts, where each individual player employs their own unique style. What's different about the Free Throw is the cadence and sequence by which each shooter shoots. As opposed to any other shot, players tend to shoot their Free Throws the exact same way each and every time, time after time, game after game, through their entire careers. You'll notice they each have their own individual way of doing what they do and they do it the same way each time. For instance, a given player will bend their knees and crouch the same way each time. They will bounce the ball in the same manner and the same amount of times prior to the shot. They'll pause for the same amount of time before extending and releasing, in the same manner each and every time.

What's interesting is the manner by which Jordan grew-up practicing his Free Throws. He took this practice to Zen like state of training. He obviously understood the concept of 'Kata'. He polished and honed his shot, so well that in a 1991 game against the Denver Nuggets, he taunted; then rival Dikembe Mutombo, by saying "Hey, Mutombo. This one's for you" He closed his eyes and sunk the shot like nobody's business and followed it up with his pearly whites as he arrogantly smiled back at Mutombo to win the game.

While there might not be some sort of 'Holy Grail', there is a method which far outweighs any of today's more common approaches. At the very least you should invest your time in learning about this approach, adopt its principles and infuse them into your training regime. Dry-Fire Training is to Shooting what the Free Throw is to basketball. If you had to choose (1) method of learning to 'Shoot' and manipulate a firearm, Dry-Fire Training or 'Snapping In' is your BEST choice.

Dry-Fire Training is how one fine tunes and hones their craft and it's the best way to win the fight ahead of time. Dry-Fire Training derives its name from the fact that the trainee presses the trigger on an empty or 'Dry' chamber, meaning there's a complete absence of ammunition. This affords you the ability to practice Trigger Manipulation without the need for ammunition, thereby completely avoiding the need for a firearms range. Just like with basketball Free Throws, all 'Time' stops. You have all the time in the world today, to isolate and perfect each and every individual element, which makes-up the overall movement or function, for that perfect shot tomorrow. You, determine how long it takes to perform said movements and how focused your attention to detail actually is. Best of all Dry-Fire Training is 'Free', can be done from home and is hands down the best way to master one's Kata.

Now I know what you're thinking, how is it possible to learn how to defend one's self with a gun, by shooting an empty one at home? Don't you need to master 'Recoil' and actually shoot at targets to know what real bullets actually do? The simple answer is, NO! All bullets do the exact same thing every single time. When the round's primer is struck by the firing pin, the primer initiates a series of controlled explosions, thereby propelling the projectile; or bullet, down the barrel. Once the projectile clears the muzzle, gravity and wind is all that matters. Like bullets, the Recoil of a given caliber of ammunition is the exact same every time in your particular firearm. When the round initiates, physics causes the energy of the explosion, to force the firearm up and back towards you at the very same rate and pitch each and every time. How you go about controlling recoil and sending an accurate round downrange has less to do about 'Shooting' and EVERYTHING to do about what you do 'Physically' to the firearm prior to the round ever being fired. Meaning, what matters most is the perfection of 'Kinesis' not making the gun go bang.

What traditional firearms training does, is attempt to teach a person to learn how to do something 'Right' by first doing something 'Wrong'. What I mean is, they take a novice to a firing range, hand them a loaded firearm, give them verbal instruction on how their supposed to 'Physically' manipulate said firearm, then tell them to "FIRE". What do you think happens? They miss. Now the instructor goes about attempting to erase the miss through further verbal instruction and has them fire again and again and again until they 'Miss' more accurately. That's what you call learning to do something wrong, expensively.

Some of the best Snipers in history come from Russia. They have consistently produced the deadliest shooters in the greatest numbers since WWI. The reason has to do with 'How' they condition their Snipers. Instead of giving them a box of ammunition and sending them to the range, they spend the vast majority of their time Dry-Firing. Then when the 'Test' comes, they're given them ONE round because the first round is the only round that matters.

When a person Dry-Fires a weapon over and over and over, their body begins to 'Feel' its way around the enigma of mastery. Dry-Fire is what breaks the code, while their body feels its way into perfect harmony of that particular firearm's mechanics and its relationship to a given person's own body mechanics. Overtime the two become one and they've become the weapon.

The difference between a Dry-Fire shooter and your typical firearms shooter is that the traditional shooter is forever plagued by recoil. Because the traditional shooter has attempted to learn how to master their firearm under the explosive influence of recoil, they're hands and intern the rest of their body has not been able to 'Feel' the relationship between the perfect grip and trigger squeeze as the firearm is in perfect alignment with their wrists, arms, shoulders and eyes. Periodically, the traditional shooter my feel one or two components of harmonious kinesis, however the effects of recoil completely prevent them from feeling all of these vital elements at once. However, the Dry-Fire shooter, simply loads their firearm, and manipulates it as though there were no bullet at all. To them, what they do 'Before' recoil is all that matters. Their bodies have already memorized how to perfectly feel it's way through the sequence of movements for that harmonious shot.

However, traditional Dry-Fire Training systems fall short and do not provide the totality of training required to master the 'Combatives' of Firearms Self-Defense. Similarly, there are a hand-full of other training methods; like the 'Four Point Draw', which delve into the concepts of Kata, but still fail to provide the density required for an actual fight. Likewise, they also fall short and don't offer a total-training-system like Japanese Aikido. Traditional approaches focus on the 'Movement' but fail to accompany said movement with 'Thought'. The result is a dull blade. Because the trainee hasn't thought their way through said movements, they haven't been able to finely hone or sharpen its edge. Sure a dull edge is better than no edge, but wouldn't you rather have the sharpest blade? Traditional Dry-Fire systems also focus on one movement, 'Trigger Presses', and completely fail to incorporate all the other components of Firearms Combatives, like Stance, Grip, Proper Alignment, Follow-Through, Loading & Re-Loading etc. In order to master Firearms Combatives, one must understand the relationship between 'Thought' and 'Kinesis' and amalgamate these into the mastery of the overall use of their firearm.

When you watch a Japanese Aikido master practice his craft, it looks much like a slow-motion choreographed dance. The reason is because he's learned the magic of marrying thought to movement. When I say 'Thought', I mean laser focused, Zen like concentration. When I say 'Movement' I mean a sloth like slow-motion, over exaggerated, individual and precise sequence of multiple variances. The Aikido warrior becomes a 'Master' of his craft by perfecting the art of 'Thinking Through' his movement's in training, so as to develop a surgically lethal orchestra of combative movement, strategically constructed to embody a given Combative Response for tomorrow's fight. Like a slug on a trail, the Master perfects their art by breaking-down the individual actions of an overall physical response, into minute forms of movement. They then go about polishing each and every individual process to arrive at a perfectly performed kinesthetic response.

To understand this better let's, explore the Japanese concept of 'Kata' which means 'Form' or in other words a particular 'From' of a physical discipline. In Japanese Martial Arts, they believe each physical discipline tells a story and each story can be choreographed into a slow-motion dance and with that dance, one can train to 'Master' their discipline.

Kata is based on (3) very important understandings:

1. The 'Structural Integrity' of that discipline.
2. The, 'Coherence' and relationship of the movements required for that discipline.

3. The overall 'Intent' behind that specific discipline.

In terms of Structural Integrity, this discipline is broken up in to a multitude of individually unique movements. Some of these movements are big, while others are small, some of them simple while others are much more complicated, some can be performed quickly while other must be done slowly and with consistent momentum. In the end, the combination of these movements and their orientation to one another, must make sense and one movement must be applicable with the next.

In terms of the Coherence of these movements, everything must flow together to appear to be, one seamless and perfectly performed action. Like water poured from a cup, each individual molecule must be perfectly adhered to the next so that from the outside, it appears the action of fighting is so perfectly complete and intact, that it resembles a cup of water's ability to be poured; which consists of millions of individual water molecules all falling, melding together to fall to the ground as 'One', at the same speed and in the same fashion.

The Intent of the discipline at hand, speaks for itself. Oddly when it relates to Firearms Self-Defense training, 99% of the methods in existence, completely ignore this all important component. The obvious intent is to 'Kill' your enemy before they kill you. The cognition of the concept of 'Killing' is completely absent at almost every firearms range known to man. Don't get me wrong, most people fully understand the end goal will likely result in someone's death, but the actual cognitive process of the 'Thought' of killing, while practicing each individual movement of shooting, is as foreign a concept as Pluto is to Mercury, on most ranges. By focusing on the intent behind the craft while training, knowing that each and every minute movement pertains to the 'Action' of 'Killing' your Threat and that the ability to 'Kill' your Threat is, completely dependent upon the combination of the overall Structural Integrity of your action and its cohesive qualities to each particular movement, requires one to take their training to a whole new level of consciousness. Its only then that a person is able to 'Master' their Combative Response through the management of their movements.

It is this art form, which enables someone to become a master of the craft of Firearms Self-Defense. While other training methods fall short, the *ZuluFight Dry-Fire Training System* is founded on the concept of 'Kata' and is the most balanced approach capable of unthinkable levels of proficiency. It's been painstakingly design to incorporate all aspects of firearms use. Through a Zen like attention to detail, the ZuluFighter is able to polish each and every aspect of firearms use, from the draw, it's presentation, manipulation, loading and reloading, malfunction mitigation, carry and shooting positions, from standing or even seated, standing idle and even moving as well as After Action Scanning techniques. There's nothing like it on the market, it's inexpensive, is performed when and where you'd like, requires no trips to the range and is the fastest way to achieve the highest level of firearms proficiency possible. It truly is a Firearms Total Training System. *ZuluFight* is a must have, an investment you simply can't go without. Turn to Page 131 to learn more about this must have system.

Stress inoculation...

Your next step in towards the development of the most squared away Self-Defense Response, is to prepare your mind for the battle ahead. The famed tactician Sun Tzu tells us to win our battles a thousand times before we ever face our enemies. When you delve into the logic behind such a simple approach to victory, you quickly understand just how daunting the task of 'Winning' actually is.

Sun Tzu realized that no matter how 'Powerful' you may be today, conflict itself has a way of wearing down even the most experienced warrior tomorrow. He fully understood the realities associated with battle, realizing that there are a number of Psychological and Physiological effects, which simply can't be avoided and which directly work against your chances of success. However, he also understood the gift of 'Strategy' and how pre-planning or war-rooming, can exponentially increase one's ability to win in spite of the odds.

In order to overcoming tomorrows torrent of stress, you must immerse yourself in the world of 'Force Science'. Force Science is the study of conflict and its effect on the human body both physically and psychologically. This is by far the MOST overlooked aspect of battle prepping for both the citizen and professional alike. I can't stress the importance of learning all you can today about what WILL happen tomorrow. In fact, I've dedicated a whole section on the subject of Force Science. You are encouraged to read and reread that section as much as possible. Gaining a solid grasp of the concepts of Force Science will afford you the Sea Legs you'll need tomorrow, when the apocalyptic tsunami; called Combat Stress, surges over you, soaking you through and through. There are ways to reinforce your foundations today, so you can weather the storm and survive the battle ahead. However, doing so requires your diligence right now, in learning and preparing yourself for the whirlwind of chaos you will face when your life is threatened.

After you've submerged yourself in the concepts of Force Science, it's time to go about inoculating yourself ahead of time. As previously mentioned, there are a number of psychological and physiological affects you will experience in Combat, which simply can't be avoided. However, there are things you can do today, to limit their effect so you can better manage the experience of them tomorrow. The best way to do this is through Force on Force scenario based training.

One of the best examples of Force on Force training can be found on the First Person Defender YouTube page. First Person Defender is a company who offers realistic Self-Defense scenario based training opportunities, which are completely free to the YouTube viewer. What makes their video's such a powerful asset, is that each scenario is played real-time from multiple camera angles, giving you the feeling of being right there, while also allowing for that third-person, outside looking in perspective. On top of this, each scenario is also debriefed and critiqued in-depth, allowing you the opportunity to learn a plethora of lessons from each and every scenario.

Force on Force training allows you the ability to see and feel the effects of Combat before the battle actually occurs. Because the roll-player is forced into a stressfully combative environment, requiring their need to make lightning quick decisions with accuracy, while also implementing an instantaneous Self-Defense Response, this experience is etched deep into their psyche. The byproduct of this etching affords your subconscious brain an ability to memorize the 'Experience' of conflict. Even though Force on Force training is, training and not a real-life fight, the level of stress is such that after only a few exposures to this type of training, a novice can quite easily approach a similar real-world occurrence with not only confidence, but with an unconscious awareness and knowhow for tomorrow's battle.

You are greatly encouraged to not only view each First Person Defender scenario, but to actually seek-out this training for yourself. Even if you attend only one class, you'll walk away light-years ahead of the game. What most people do is seek range based Tactical course. They do so with the full expectation that at least a portion of the training, will be retained and later used should their lives actually be threated. Unfortunately, until you're 'Brain' has experienced some sort of Force on Force scenario incorporating what you've learned on the range, you WON'T employ those tactics tomorrow. That is unless you have the time and money to send every day for three years, attending high-speed tactical training like a Navy SEAL. In which case your 'Brain' would have found a way to etch said training for an instantaneous response tomorrow. Trust me, you NEED to attend as many Force on Force classes as possible. Take the time and invest the money.

Another way to inoculate yourself for tomorrow's battle is by adopting a 'What When Mentality'. Don't settle for a passive; "If this happens, then I'll do that" type of approach for tomorrow's attack. Instead, develop an adherence to the concept of, 'Not If But When.' Don't merely own a firearm for 'If' something should happen. Rather, actively possess it for WHEN your life WILL be threatened and WHEN you WILL be forced to use it, to protect yourself and someone else. It's this mindset that immediately thrusts you into a whole new world of mental preparation. I'm not suggesting you become paranoid of the world around you. However, I am compelling you to prepare for whatever WILL be thrown your way. If you prepare for the worst-case scenario and devise a few practical ways of defeating such an obstacle, then anything less than that should be easily overcome. It's a bit like resistance training. If you train yourself to lift a heavy weight, then pretty soon the lighter ones feel like feathers. The more you lift the fitter you become and the fitter you are, the more capable you are for the challenge.

The 'What When Mentality' translates into: "when I'm confronted by someone while I exit my front door" and "when I'm walking to my car in a dark parking garage and I'm attacked from behind" and "when I'm sitting on my couch and I'm startled by the front door being kicked in" and "when I'm at a stoplight and am confronted by a man with a gun at my driver side window" and "when I'm at the mall with my kids and see a man with a rifle killing people left and right" or "when out at a sports bar enjoying drinks with my friends and a stranger picks a fight with me." These are examples of the depth by which you must take your thought and for each 'When' you need to take the time to formulate at least three different ways of overcoming such an occurrence.

Remember, tomorrow's fight WILL be a reaction to an attack that's already underway. This means you're already behind the 8-Ball. It may also occur at ranges within arm's reach. In cases like this, you may have to either fight 'To' your weapon, or even forgo the use of your firearm altogether and settle for a hands-on defense. Regardless, what you do today to inoculate yourself for tomorrow's unavoidable obstacles, makes all the difference.

Tactics...

One of the biggest errors people make when it comes to firearms training, is that they rely too heavily on Range based training. What I mean is they wrongly assume that by either going to a firearms range to shoot or that by attending a Range based class, that they will somehow walk away a more capable fighter. Sadly, they couldn't be more wrong. I've trained side-by-side with countless individuals, who underwent the very same high-speed, low-drag, uber sexy tactical schools as I, and seen them freeze in the face of a real fight.

Just because you've attended some cool training, and just because you were the star trainee who walked away with the highest scores, doesn't mean you're ready for tomorrow. Unless your tactical training is based and built upon the previous mentioned foundation of Firearms Kata and Stress Inoculation, you're doomed for failure and all you're doing is wasting valuable time and money.

What you should do is spend the time to build a solid foundation of understanding. Then reinforce that foundation by conditioning your body and mind to Master the tools you plan on bring to the battle. It's not until you've gained a high level of proficiency in the actual use; or shall I say manipulation, of your weapon, that actual Range based training becomes useful.

Once you have gained an acceptable level of proficiency and can, load, unload, clear malfunctions and manipulate your trigger without having to stop and think about what to do, then it's time to seek actual 'Tactical Training'. There are a ton of so called 'Experts' out there. Do your homework and don't just settle on one, find a two or three instructors who know what they're talking about. There is power in diversity of training, it makes that 'Edge' even sharper and gives you multiple trains of thought to overcome the same problem.

2
So What is Force Science?

Force Science is the study of the most extreme forms of physical conflict between humans known as 'Deadly Force Encounters'. Force Science dissects the dynamics associated with Combat to identify and measure physiological and psychological effects, which may be common from one person to another.

Force Science is a frailly new discipline, which began in the early 1970s. The intent was twofold:

1. The Special Operations Community wanted to find ways to increase a warfighters' overall potency on the battlefield and identify ways to pass this on to the regular army.

2. Top military brass were concerned with the overwhelming number of service members returning from Vietnam, who suffered from extreme psychological disorders. The extremely high numbers of Psych Casualties were most alarming and far greater than any previous conflict. They wanted to figure out what if anything had changed; in terms of Combat, and exactly how Combat; itself, effected the average warfighter.

The long and short is that scientists found exactly what they were searching for, but they also uncovered a treasure trove of information that's completely changed how we approach Combat today. However, it took some time for scientist, psychologist and doctors to catch up to a whole new way of thinking.

Twenty years later; in the 1990s, two main groups took this research to a whole new level and made it the science we know today. KILLOLOGY RESEARCH GROUP and the FORCE SCIENCE INSTITUTE ® are two completely independent and unbiased-based groups comprised of scientists, doctors, psychologist and tactical experts, who focus on the physiological and psychological effects of Deadly Force Encounters. Man has been in Combat since Cane and Able, yet astonishingly, the 'Science' behind Combat has been pretty much hit and miss, (pun intended) until the advent of the above mentioned groups.

They were the first to connect the dots and fill in the gaps from the more archaic research of the 1970s. They were able to identified patterns and extrapolate probable outcomes to give us a much better understand of exactly what to expect when we're faced with a deadly threat. What their research has found tells us that we've been doing it wrong all along. Sadly, we've been training to LOSE not to win.

Combat Gravity...

If there is one thing the study of Force Science has revealed, it would be that there exists a myriad of unavoidable and common effects, which everybody experiences. Combat itself has a very distinct impact on how a person will actually physically respond while threatened. This impact is vastly different than how a person acts under ANY other circumstances, other than during the most extreme life or death situations. The sum of these effects represent what I call the 'Laws of Combat'. These laws can be likened to Sir Isaac Newton's 'Laws of Physics'. The mere existence of Combat, has a measurable and defined effect on man. Regardless of race, nationality, gender or physical composition, there are a handful of common effects of Combat, which cannot be averted.

Think of it in terms of 'Gravity'. Everybody knows the effect of gravity when it relates to our ability to maneuver here on Earth. It's what keeps our feet to the ground, our constant. In the same way, Combat has its own gravitational force. There are physiological and psychological realties that affect every man, woman or child who experiences Combat.

The reality is that we all experience extremely similar effects during a struggle for our existence. While each individual effect is not guaranteed, every human being engaged in Combat, will experience the majority of them to one extreme or another. While these effects are completely unavoidable, their influence can be dramatically reduced to a much more manageable degree. Science has shown that we can pre-condition our minds and in turn our bodies; beforehand, to experience 'Combat Gravity' with less overall effect on our ability to navigate its waters.

An analogy of this concept can be derived from the conditioning an Astronaut undergoes prior to their travel into outer space. Over a life of experiencing the effects of Gravity here on Earth, their bodies have developed their own harmonic balance. If abruptly thrust into space and placed on the Moon, a person would experience great discomfort and fear without proper preparation, since they would end up bouncing from one side to the other. To this day Astronauts practice simulated Low Gravity Training, so they're adequately prepared for the effects of said Gravity on the Moon or Space in general. Something as simple as drinking water in Space, can be a very daunting task and extremely difficult to complete while in Space. Yet on Earth this most basic function, which most of us master by the age of (4), is taken for granted here on Earth. Similar basic physical functions associated with using a firearm while under attack, are just as much an out-of-this-world experience as drinking water from a cup, in an almost zero gravity environment like that of the International Space Station.

Just as the Moon is a world away from our experiences here on Earth, Combat is as distant our everyday lives as Mars or better yet Pluto. In the same way, Force Science has shown that anyone can prep for tomorrow's battle and develop natural responses to afford them the most positive outcome.

An example on how poor training can completely sabotage one's ability to win during the 'Act' of Combat, can be found in something as simple as how they stand during training. Stance is one of the most overlooked aspects of firearms training, yet it provides the entire base for your Physical Response. For the most part people initially acquire a stance that looks tactical cool like the 'Isosceles Stance'. But soon and usually within a few short minutes, their stance becomes more of a flat-footed, weight on heals Weaver Stance. What happens is they lose focus of the 'Crouch' and forward lean required for an effective Isosceles Stance and quickly get tired due to muscle fatigue. What results is the entirety of the rest of their training is performed from a completely different base, which completely effects overall accuracy. The laziness and poor habitual manner of their stance in training, is then encoded in their brain as Muscle Memory through the procedural aspects of their training.

Interestingly, Force Science research clearly shows that EVERYONE who actually perceives an immediately attacking lethal threat, will instinctively assume a squatted crouch, identical to that of the Modified Isosceles shooting stance. No matter how well you've training and no matter how elite your profession may be, this is latterly an innate physical reaction that CAN'T be overridden. A great example of this can be seen in the video footage of then President Reagan's attempted assassination on March 30th 1981. During this real-world deadly attack EVERY single individual is seen assuming an 'Oh Shi Crouch' directly proceeding John Hinckley Junior's initial shots.

What's even more interesting is that each and every person immediately present did the same exact thing regardless of their previous training or their current physical responsibility. From reporter, to staff, to regular police officers to the elite team of Reagan's Secret Service Detail, each and every person crouched and maintained that crouch throughout their following Physical Response. Remember, members of a Secret Serve Presidential Security Detail, undergo a degree of unheard of pre-training and continued training that could easily be likened to the practice of a Religion. Even with all their training, each Secret Service member crouched in the same fashion and even paused for about the same amount of time, prior to putting into motion their Defensive Response.

The reality is that during attack you WILL assume a 'Modified Isosceles Stance' throughout the incident regardless of your previous training. If Force Science has proven that this is as much of a reality as Gravity is to the Law of Physics, then why do so many people waste so much time shooting from a Weaver or any other type of shooting stance? Your shooting stance is your 'Base' it determines and galvanizes the overall integrity of all other aspects of fighting which shooting is but 'One' portion. Maintaining proper stance through the entirety of your training will assure that all the other physical movements you hone during that training evolution, are not wasted and are built on a sure foundation that's consistent with the Laws of Combat and don't attempt to defy the Laws of Physics. Understanding something so simple yet so vitally important as 'Stance' during training, highlights just why an adequate grasp of the topic of Force Science is so essential if you want to 'Win' tomorrow's battle. Winning is first accomplished through the 'pre'-study of conflict.

The mind, a terrible thing to waste...

Our brains define us and set us apart from all other living beings. The totality, function and overall capabilities they offer are inconceivable. Neuroscientists are still uncovering the secrets and wonder behind how our brains develop and function. Our brains are truly our greatest asset. Yet, in times of great crisis they can often become our greatest obstacle.

Force Science researchers have consistently shown that our ability to manage 'Combat Stress' is directly derived from how our minds process the concepts of this stress beforehand. It's all about pre-conditioning. In fact, our success is completely dependent upon our mind's ability to formulate an instantaneous response absent cognitive thought. Just as our brain's continually cause our lungs to expand and contract without thought, so too must we have a pre-wired solution for tomorrow's battle. This starts by understanding the processes of our physiology and psychology and how they're affected during Combat. Similar to how an Olympic Athlete utilizes Hyperbaric Chamber Training to pre-condition their lungs for the extreme stressors of such a high level of competition, so too must you pre-condition the physiology and psychology of your mind for Combat.

Fight, Flight or Freeze...

Over the course of our lives, our brains have subconsciously developed one of three instantaneous responses to an immediate and deadly threat. We will either 'Fight' our Threat with all our might, 'Flee' from it as fast as humanly possible or we will completely shut down and 'Freeze' like a deer caught in the headlights. This is also known as 'Combat Paralysis', which can last anywhere from seconds or minutes and can easily lead to a medical state of shock.

Our brains are designed to develop and operate on two parallel planes. During times of grave danger and when faced with a threat to our very existence, our brains revert back to the most primitive forms of function.

1. The most common plane, I like to call the 'Intelligent Brain'. It's where we live 99.99% of our lives. It's the cognitive and intellectually creative form of us. This operation is achieved through the cooperative interaction of our Prefrontal Cortex with both our brain's right and left hemispheres.

    - To better understand this, our Intelligent Brain is like our desktop computer. It's comprised of all that makes our computer different than the next. It is made up of its operating system and background functions, the main hard-drive, auxiliary drives and the multitude of custom software suites.

2. The more primitive plane is much different than our Intelligent Brain. I call this the 'Caveman Brain' or the Amygdala. It's mainly comprised of all our basic body functions; the innate processes our brain makes on its own, which maintain all 11 basic body function systems, like those of our nervous and circulatory

systems. It also consists of an extremely small sampling of our Intelligent Brain's ability to problem solve.

- To better understand this, our Caveman Brain is like our desktop computer's master default, the archaic DOS or C Prompt. No Windows OS, no software, just code.

- Many so called Tactical Experts have training methods which fall apart during real-life Combat because they designed their methods on an Intellectual footing requiring the use of one's 'Intelligent' cognitive brain function. However, during the polar shift of Combat; where our brains revert back to Caveman function, all those 'Intellectual' possesses go out the window. In Combat you're left with basic computer code, while all those fancy dancy high-tech tactical sexy software applications end up crashing. What you should be doing is learning to be a Combat Computer IT Analyst because that's exactly what you'll need when someone tries to kill you tomorrow and you're faced with the complexities of the unavoidable Combat Computer Code Crash.

Due to genetics and early childhood influences, our Caveman Brains accumulate a mixture of automated responses which are immediately fired when faced with grave danger. This is that small sampling of intellectual problem solving discussed above. When faced with a problem our Caveman Brain throws an extremely primitive solution at it. It really is basic Addition & Subtraction though; it's nowhere near the level of Trigonometry or even Basic Algebra. These automated, pre-programmed, responses are completely innate and instinctive. They're an instantaneous function requiring almost zero cognitive processing whatsoever.

Similar to our body's homeostasis; how it regulates and maintains the perfect PH balance, our brains develop their own form of psychoneuro-homeostasis. Over a lifelong of external influences and experiences, our brains establish a physiological and physiological balance. When balanced, this state of being enables our Intelligent Brains to function with ease in relation to the world around us. However, when faced with impending death, this balance is violently thrown upside-down. At that moment our Caveman Brain floods our systems with a cocktail of the most potent hormones and chemicals. The effects of this mind altering chemical cocktail greatly affects our body's response to the perceived Threat and ultimately determines our overall ability to respond to the Threat(s) or whether we Fight, Flee or end-up Freeze.

Top Secret...

When faced with a deadly threat to our very existence, our brains feverishly search for a folder titled 'Top Secret'. This folder holds the solution to our immediate problem. The trouble arises when our brains experiences the polar shift; mentioned previously, as it goes from using the Intelligent Brain to our primitive Caveman Brain. It's at that moment when our secretary; our brain's Amygdala, grabs the first folder she can get her hands on and throws it at the problem. The probability that she will retrieve the particular individual folder, which contains your specifically tailored solution for that particular problem, is completely dependent upon how you've already organized, correlated and filed that folder beforehand. When it comes to the use of a weapon in response to an attacking threat; how you respond, is completely dependent upon the degree and quality of Procedural Memory Encoding you've performed beforehand.

Our brains are like huge storage vaults capable of storing a life's long accumulation of information and experiences. For the most part we organize these banks of information in similar fashion to that of a filing system. For Combat experts, this system is as sophisticated as the vault like industrial catalogs like those you'd find at a courthouse or museum.

Most people however, file their information in a much less technical manner. This would more closely resemble an everyday two drawer filing cabinet. Over time our brains develop habits of storage, utilizing different kinds of coding and correlating. Some folders are red while others are blue. Some folders go to the top drawer while others live in the bottom. Some are situated to the left while others are stored to the right. In an everyday world; while experience everyday experiences with low stress, your Intelligent Brain can typically locate nearly any folder by memory of where it was last stored. This is due to the process of Cognitive Thought, which is the brain's overall cooperative effort of all its parts.

Ninety-nine point nine-nine percent of Westerners live their lives in an ultra-state of peace. In fact, most Westerners will go a lifetime without being physically confronted let alone have someone actually try and kill them. It's important to understand this because just as our Intelligent Brain develops habits of process, our Caveman Brain does as well. The brain is a muscle and like any muscle, if it's not used, it becomes weak. The down side to our peace filled lives is that our Caveman Brain hardly if ever gets its workout in. So when death comes knocking, our Amygdala is left with the daunting task of finding that 'One' perfect solution for an out-of-this-world problem, amongst the clutter of all the other files, piled up around her. This is where the right kind of training makes all the difference and is precisely why the 'Right' kind of training is so essential.

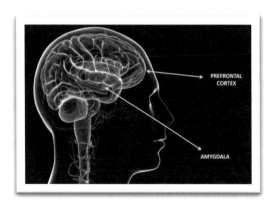

Our Intelligent Brain utilizes the vastness of the Prefrontal Cortex; which is about the size of your fist, to calculate its solutions for the world around it. In contrast, our Caveman Brain uses an area the size of a pea, the Amygdala. That tiny, barely legible portion of the otherwise vastness of the rest of our brain, that's what our Caveman Brain uses to formulate its response to a Deadly Encounter. That tiny, insignificant dot is the most significantly momentous apparatuses in your entire body. This is what <u>WILL</u> determine how you respond to deadly threats. Placing the 'Right' information in an appropriately marked folder during training and storing it in the proper spot, that's what will make all the difference tomorrow. It's this tiny portion of our brain; the Amygdala, that has become the focal point of Force Science. It's this extremely miniscule region of the human brain which gets all the attention. Your ability to overcome tomorrow's deadly threat is dependent upon how well you understand this process and how well you 'Condition' and encode a pre-programmed response. Proper conditioning is only achieved through proper training. However, it's not just about 'Training' but the 'Right' kind of training makes this possible.

Most of us place the cart before the horse. We spend a small fortune on that perfect gun, which by all means is guaranteed to stop any bad guy dead in his tracks, right? Wrong! From time to time we set out on a pilgrimage to Tactical Mecca, where we hewn and ready our hands for battle by plinking at cardboard silhouettes or even glass bottles. We then return home and go about our lives as normal. Rarely do we ever actually take the time to stop and 'Think Through' the physiology and psychology of conflict. Neurologists go to school first. Ninety-five percent of their time is spent in books and lecture halls before they ever touch a human brain, let alone begin to cut into one. The kinesis of battle is useless if your brain hasn't been conditioned in the process of selecting the appropriate Tactical Response under the extreme stresses of Combat.

Taking the time to study Force Science and memorizing the scientific Laws of Combat will pay dividends tomorrow. Learning first what your body WILL do, will save you from spending tons of wasted time at the firearms range, inadvertently conditioning and encoding the 'Wrong' tactics for the wrong response.

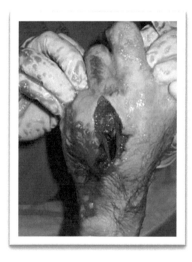

Warning Apocalyptic Tsunami Ahead!!!

What's all the hype about? What's the big deal? You're ready you say? Oh yes, because you have a 1911 .45 ACP by your side at all times. You're ready for anything....

The truth? Physical confrontations with firearms is the most fluidly dynamic environment you will ever know. The overwhelming and unavoidable tidal wave of physiological and psychological effects, rates up there with an Apocalyptic Tsunami. Armed confrontations aren't action movies or video games and they're no 3 Gun match. There are no do-overs and EVERY error is immediately accompanied by a devastatingly lethal consequence.

Most armed citizens foolishly assume they're defensive firearms abilities are suffice. Many think that because they grew-up around firearms, carry one everywhere they go or because they're an expert 3 Gun competitor; they actually believe whole heartedly, they're ready for Combat. The problem lays in their ignorance of 'Fact' and of the unavoidable troubles which lurk ahead. They simply have no clue of the deluge that will wash over them like the worst kind of tidal wave imaginable. They aren't prepared for, or even aware of, the concept of 'Combat Gravity' nor are have the conditioned themselves to react appropriately in spite of the apocalyptic effects of Combat Stress. For instance:

Action vs. Reaction:

1. The average untrained attacker can achieve a (90%) hit ratio on their prey, while the average untrained defender can only achieve upwards of around a (17-20%) hit ratio in response?

2. Statistics show that 90% of real-world shootings involve multiple rounds being fired and the average untrained person can shoot (4) rounds per-second. That's right, I said an "Untrained" person can shoot (4) rounds per-second.

3. Action is <u>ALWAYS</u> faster than reaction, it's a scientific fact. It takes the average human (0.30) seconds to simply react to a change in their environment. That's merely identifying the existence of 'Change', NOT reacting to said change. Now begins the daunting task of 'Reaction'. Given the overwhelming Stress Cocktail associated with any deadly attack, it takes a minimum of (0.53) more seconds to overcome and process the initial shock & awe of that attack. Then after all that; at (0.83) seconds, you can actually begin to implement some type of a physical response. Meaning, it's not until (0.83) seconds into the fight that your brain tells your hand to move towards your holster.

4. Now consider the totality of the relationship between Action vs. Reaction, physics and your ability to survive the attack. The problem presented is a bad guy who's threatened or is actually using a gun against you. You're already drastically behind the Eight Ball. To survive you must identify the Threat, formulate a response, and then implement said response. As mentioned previously you're likely to sustain between (6.52 – 10.88) hits before you send your first round. If you don't believe this statistic, YouTube the 1981 President Reagan Assassination Attempt. You'll see that John Hinckley Jr. was able to get (6) rounds off, before some of the World's most highly trained and capable individuals were able to finally subdue him.

5. This real-world Deadly Encounter is a perfect example because it gives you a snapshot of the cross-section of tactically minded persons present, from the horribly inept reporters and advisors and press sectaries to the elite of the elite Secret Service Presidential Detail members. It took each of these people so much time to respond that John Hinckley Jr. was able to shoot (6) times in (1.7) seconds, standing (10) feet away from President Reagan. His first shot was a headshot of all things. Four of his (6) shots hit multiple people including Reagan all before he could be subdued. It's only certain Reagan would have been hit more would he not have had an entourage of people immediately present to protect his life. You can rest assure, you WON'T have a Secret Service Detail protecting you when you're attacked.

6. Remerging that bullets don't discriminate between right or wrong, friend or foe, victim or criminal, the reality is that molten hot, razor-sharp, metal objects will likely tare through your body at nearly 1,200 fps. This will cause profuse bleeding and immediately begin the ultimate shutdown of the majority of your overall bodily functions. It's only after this, that science shows that you're humanly capable to draw your weapon and begin the uphill battle of defending your life. Does that concern you? Does it make your stomach turn? It most certainly should. This is why the 'Right' kind of training makes all the difference beforehand.

Close Quarters Battles (C.Q.B.) / Proximity to Threat:

1. Distance equals time. The shorter the distance the less time one has to perceive an attack, react and then overcome the perceived deadly attack.

2. Distance also affects accuracy. Since you're reacting to attack, proximity is NOT your friend. The closer your Threat is, the less accurate he needs to be to achieve lethal hits. If your Threat is completely inept at 25 yards and couldn't even place one round on paper, at two or three feet, it's entirely possible that he'll score a possible and each of his rounds will rip through you before you even react.

3. At close proximity a number of other factors are immediately present. For instance, you can touch, feel, smell and even taste your Threat. The aroma of his body odor, the clamminess of his skin, the perplexing and paralyzing gaze of his lifeless thousand-yard stare. An up close and personal struggle for life with another human being is simply unmatched. It's daunting, spooky and emotionally unsettling even for the most experienced among us.

The Stress Cocktail:

1. **Fear (The Human Phobia of Death):** The greatest most unavoidable innate reaction to a deadly threat is our natural fear of death. While some can learn to dilute and decrease the effect of this reaction, most people will be thrust into a whirlwind of paralyzing fear. Lt. Col. Dave Grossman coined it "The Human Phobia of Death." Like any of our most extreme phobias; spiders, snakes or heights, our entire being will immediately be galvanized. It will be like getting struck by lightning. Potent chemicals and hormones, like adrenalin and dopamine, will flood our bloodstream. The effects of which will throw your brain into an ultra DEFCON 1 level of security lockdown. From here, only the bodily functions required to perceive the Threat, determine an immediate response and then react to said Threat, will function. Everything else goes on lockdown. You simply revert back to the Caveman Brain where the only thing that matters is survival. It's at this moment that you will either Fight, Flee or Freeze. Sadly, most freeze, bring unavoidable death.

2. **Heart Rate Explosion:** An adults normal resting heart rate lives anywhere between (60-80) bpm. Optimal competitive function lives between (115-145) bpm. At this range you're afforded the perfect combination of blood & oxygen flow throughout your body, which enables optimal performance of your entire system. However, for the average citizen who's never faced an actual deadly attack, it's entirely possible for your heart rate to spike between (180-220) bpm or even higher. This is a very dangerous range. Even during normal everyday exercise, like running on a treadmill, if maintained over an extended period of time, this can easily cause cardiac arrest. This range is CATASTROPHIC while in heated battle. Due to the presence of the abnormally high levels of dangerous chemicals, the tidal wave of adrenalin and dopamine; which is violently pumping through you, if your heart rate isn't brought back to a safe level, cardiac arrest can occur within seconds as opposed to minutes. Even if you avoid cardiac arrest, at this range your body teeters between

Conditions Gray & Black, meaning you're on the verge of total physical shutdown, like an engine seizing from a lack of oil.

3. **Loss of Peripheral Vision:** This is known as 'Focused Vision' or 'Tunnel Vision'. During attack the ONLY thing you will see is what you need to see. The color of the leaves on a distant tree, the little old lady crossing the street, or even the gigantic skyscraper standing directly behind the person trying to kill you. These are all irrelevant and will likely be completely erased from your perceived vision. This can be a good thing as it will give you a laser beam like, focused type of clarity of your Threat, but what if you're attacked by two or more individuals? Or what about when you consider your response and begin to fire back? Where are your rounds going to go should they miss? Will they hit the little old lady crossing the street? Or the family quietly eating their lunch in the restaurant directly behind your Threat?

4. Loss of Near Vision: Think about this, if you can't see your sights because your eyes simply can't see them; due to the fact that your eyes are ONLY trained on that which is trying to actively kill you, how are you going to use your sights to hit your Threat? While under attack, your eyes will see only what they need to see. Because your sights aren't trying to kill you, your eyes won't see them. Again, all your eyes car about is focusing on whomever or whatever it straying to kill you. This sort of phasing out of non-threatening objects is also true for other objects or non-treating people within the spectrum of your near vision.

5. **Loss of Depth Perception:** We rely on our ability to decipher depth in relation to our proximity to objects and surfaces around us. A drastic loss of this important sense would be like trying to fight while experiencing vertigo. Not knowing the true distance to objects in your immediate environment, increases the likelihood that you will trip or stumble, making you completely vulnerable and useless during attack. Understanding this now can help to elevate moments of panic should this occur during your fight.

6. **Auditory Exclusion:** As a result of the perceived likelihood of death, you may experience a temporary loss of hearing. Similar to 'Focused Vision', your ears will be trained on your Threat and will completely block out the plethora of sounds in your environment. A good example of this is best understood by those who've ever hunting before. When they raise their rifle and shoot their game, the report of the rifle sounds like a muffled pop-gun and their hearing is hardly affected. Yet shooting that same rifle on the range absent hearing protection would leave their ears ringing in pain. Much of this is due to the high levels of adrenaline and dopamine that will surge through your body. In a real gunfight you'll likely experience the same kinds of auditory effects, where everything but your Threat appears muffled.

7. **Loss of Fine Motor Skills:** We rely on Fine Motor Skills for everything. In many ways it's what separates us from primates. Our ability to thread a needle provides the clothing on our backs. Our ability to put thought to paper, by holding a small pen to artistically communicate thoughts and ideas on paper, affords us the ability to expand our understanding. This fine motor skill alone; manipulating a pen to put thoughts on paper, provides blueprints of success for our children and our children's children. Our abilities to finely manipulate our bodies enables us to dominate our environment. However, while under deadly attack, your physiological system is taken out of balance and you will lose the ability to do simple physical things. Under these situations you're left with trying to force a square peg through a round hole or sinking a small nail on a wall with a 20 lb. sledgehammer.

8. **The Slow Motion Effect:** A well-known phenomenon, which effects most people who experience extreme high levels of stress during deadly attack, is perceived slow motion. Time itself appears to literally come to a halt and barely ticks by. The best way to articulate this is to compare it to the scene in the movie 'The Matrix' where Neo dodges the torrent of bullets being fired at him, while he bends backwards and manipulates his body here and there, dodging every slow moving bullet slicing through the air. Similarly, time will appear to slow so much so that your movements may appear to be a sort of out-of-body experience.

9. **The Hyper Speed Effect:** Another phenomenon is the sense that your world has just jumped into a hyper speed wormhole. Sometimes people experience a weird mixture of the two where they experience a most bewildering tug-of-war of some outside force randomly pulling them from hyper speed to slow motion and back. A good example of this is seen in the movie 'Contact' when Dr. Ellie Arroway shoots through the Space Time Continuum and is violently torn from one world to the next. At one moment she sits in the harnessed seat of her spherical time machine. Then without warning, she's pulled up and out of the machine, looking down at herself from a God like third person view. For some people, a deadly attack can cause a very similar disturbing state of psychoses.

10. **Tormenting Thoughts:** Another extremely common effect from this type of stress is an onslaught of horribly vulgar and disturbing thoughts. For some they see their life latterly pass before their eyes as if they were sitting in a movie theater; eating popcorn, while they quickly reach the climatic and tragic end of their life story. For others it's as crazy as the most exotic acid trip causing insane hallucinations. For instance, during one of my Deadly Force incidents, I swear I saw the suspect's vehicle turn into Magnetron, as it sped towards me, spilling sparks from its wheels which looked like waves of fire. A buddy of mine later explained to me that during one of his shootings, he saw a little green Leprechaun who

continually taunted him throughout the gunfight telling him, "You're gonna dieeee…. You're gonna dieeee…" These kinds of psychotic trips can make it extremely difficult to maintain effective situational awareness and decipher truth from fiction.

11. **Loss of Bowel & Bladder Control:** This is probably something you never thought of when considering how you'll respond to a deadly attack on your life. The reality is our bodies will react absent cognitive thought. At that moment there is only one goal in mind, survival. Average normal bodily functions will go on lockdown, providing ample energy and blood flow for those organs which are needed to provide the essential functions to secure survival. This means if you have a full bladder or are close to passing your last meal, it's entirely possible that you will do so right then and there.

Combat Hydraulics…

Hopefully this chapter underlined the fact that Combat is the most chaotically charged, out of control, consistently fast moving environment known to man. Its hydrostatic qualities are measured in thousandths of seconds multiplied by pounds per square inch. The fluidity of this environment is as volatile as the ocean tide and as random as the ebb and flow of its surge. Sure you might be a competent swimmer in the backyard pool. Hell, you may even be able to hold your breath under water for 5-minutes. Surviving the converging surge in the Straits of Magellan; where the Atlantic and Pacific meet, without a life vest or a wetsuit, that takes a level of proficiency I'd be willing to bet you don't have and Combat is easily as tumultuous as converging oceans.

The act of defending one's self with a firearm is a daunting task even for professionals. However, Combat can be tamed. You may have zero experience and have never actually been in a fight for your life before. You're Caveman Brain my even be pre-wired to Freeze. You may actually be the worst fighter in the entire universe, but don't lose hope. There are ways to pre-condition practical lifesaving responses and encode them deep within your brain's primitive DOS / C Prompt command. There are things you can do today so you can WIN tomorrow's battle and live to tell about it. It starts here, by preparing your mind for how your body WILL be affected. After this you can develop kinesthetic, Tactical Responses which can be performed in spite of these effects. It's only after you fully understand these scientific realities that you can begin to develop a practical solution that actually works in a real-life gunfight.

My hopes are that this in-depth glimpse into the study of Force Science gives you the knowledge you'll need to develop both a tactical and legal response to Self-Defense. Remember, the vast majority of people haven't a clue about these realities and this includes the Judge, Jury and even your attorney. It's up to you to make this an integral part of your Defense strategy, so you can educate those involved and assure that you're not left being wrongly convicted for something that's completely out of your control.

3
The Law

To shoot or not to shoot, a most ambiguous question with no hard fast answer. Surprisingly though your decision, is something you'd probably not expect. In all reality, when faced with a deadly threat to your existence, your decision to shoot or not, will completely come down to how well you've already prepared your mind long before that fateful day. You see when you're faced with a threat to your existence, your ability to 'Reason' goes out the window. During the intellectual polar shift; as your

Caveman Brain takes over, you WILL respond however you've been conditioned to respond. It's vital that you take the time today, to pre-select the right solutions and earmark them as 'Top Secret'.

The problem with failing to take the time today, to think 'Through' possible outcomes tomorrow, arises when it comes time to judge your actions. Since judgment WILL be based on how 'Reasonable' your actions appear, your instinctive response must somehow fall on the side of reason. But how can you reason something without stopping to think? The

answer is really quite simple, 'What When?'. The advantages of war-rooming possible Self-Defense scenarios today, affords you the ability to leverage possible responses, so they're both tactically and legally sound. Taking full advantage of your ability to 'Think' today, slowing down to take the 'Time' right now to calculate the most reasonable and most tactical solutions, means when you're attacked tomorrow and there is not time, your instantaneous response to a completely chaotic occurrence, will have already been vetted and you'll select a bulletproof solution which will stand the test of both Criminal and Civil Court.

So what is the Law?

Self-Defense laws are extremely broad and the basis by which they're weighed, is completely depended upon the 'Perceived Actions' of another and how those assumed actions threaten another's wellbeing. For instance, if you're sitting quietly in your seat at a movie theater and someone walks up and punches you in the face, you may or may not be justified in shooting them. It depends on the Totality-of-the-Circumstances.

Or in other words:

1. Did you sustain injury?

2. Are you light headed, dazed or on the verge of losing consciousness?

3. Is the aggressor still an Active Threat even after the initial punch?

4. Could the aggressor's next punch cause life-threatening injury?

5. Are you trapped or confined leaving you with no reasonable way to flee?

6. Are you in fear for your life or someone else's?

These are only a few extremely important factors which help determine justification. If the answer is a resounding YES!!! to these questions, then you MIGHT be justified in the use of a firearm against an otherwise unarmed attacker. Notice I said 'Might'. Under different circumstances however, Deadly Force may NOT be justified.

These are precisely the kinds of questions presented to a 72 year-old retired cop who shot and killed an unarmed man during an altercation at a movie theater in Florida. He was arrested and charged with Second Degree Murder. His bail was set at a whopping $150,000. This meant unless he could somehow come up with hard cash, he would fight for his innocence behind bars until his trial concluded. As of the writing of this book, nearly two years have passed since this incident and his trial has still not been set. Could you come up with $150,000 today? Can you imagine the continued cost beyond this just to defend your innocence much less the stress you'd be enduring while waiting for trial? Keep in mind, a trial like this, with over twenty-two witnesses, could drag on for months, so it's completely feasible that this man won't learn his fate for another year. This; my friend, is only the Criminal aspect. When it comes to Civil Liability, I can guarantee the family of the man killed, will most certainly bring a Wrongful Death suit against him and by the looks of it, he's in for a whole other world of SUCK.

So when attempting to decode 'The Law' don't expect it to give you a definitive justified action for a particular set of circumstances. It's also very important to understand that there are a multitude of State and Federal laws, which directly relate to weapons, conduct and Self-Defense. There are also many Municipal and County codes and ordnances, which also come into play. All of these will play a pivotal role in determining whether your actions are truly justified or not.

To better understand a few VERY important concepts, let's explore some basic legal definitions pertaining to Use of Force. Keep in mind it is essential that you refer to your particular Stat's actual legal definitions as they may differ slightly from State to State.

Justified Physical Force...

"A private citizen is justified in using Physical Force for Self-Defense or the defense of a third party, from what the person reasonably believes to be the use or imminent use of unlawful Physical Force. This person is justified in using the degree of Physical Force which that person reasonably believes to be necessary for the purpose of stopping the other person's unlawful actions."

Deadly Physical Force

"Physical Force that under the circumstances in which it is used, is readily capable of causing serious physical injury."

Justified Deadly Physical Force

"A private citizen is justified in using Deadly Physical Force for Self-Defense or the defense of a third party if that person reasonably believes another person is using or about to use Unlawful Deadly Physical Force."

Serious Physical Injury

"Physical injury which creates a substantial risk of death."

Reasonable

"Agreeable to sound judgment and logic, does not exceed the limits of prescribed reason, is rational and is not excessive."

Clear as mud?

Did you notice how vague these definitions actually are? For instance, the justified use of both Physical and Deadly Force are completely based on the word 'Reasonable'. It couldn't get more ambiguous than that. Reasonableness is what I call a 'Lukewarm Word'. It's neither here nor there, up or down, left or right. Yet, it's the foundation of our entire Judicial System. The scale which Lady Justice holds in her hands, is a symbol of this concept. It speaks to the balance of reason. Is said action or perception of that action, feasible, plausible, prudent, rational and or sensible? This is where the importance of philosophical articulation comes into play. Reasonableness is derived from your ability to describe the Totality-of-the-Circumstances including what you saw, assumed and why you did what you did, in a manner that's palatable to the naysayer. To win, her scale must balance.

Similarly, Deadly Physical Force and Serious Physical Injury are also based on ambiguity. The concepts of 'Readily Capable' and 'Substantial Risk' are both subject to opinion and perspective. One could easily argue that a punch to the face does NOT justify the use of Deadly Physical Force. However, if for instance you articulate the fact that the offender appeared to be much larger than you and that his punch left you in a daze. If you also articulated that you were in a vulnerable position with no way out and that the offender was able to use all his weight with each of his punches; since he was standing above, you. If you believed it likely and feared that he would continue his course of action, then one could easily argue why Deadly Physical Force is justified, even if the offender is completely unarmed.

To sum things up, Justified Use of Force is a balanced perspective of how you view something and if your point-of-view is sensible to another reasonable person. If it is, then your Use of Force was justified. The amount and type of Physical Force is also a balance of objective viewpoints. If you are defending against something that could actually kill you, then you can use Deadly Physical Force in return. However, if another person's actions would not likely cause death, then you're limited and ONLY justified in using the amount of Physical Force which is necessary and capable of bringing a stop to the attack or control over your aggressor.

Protecting property...

So you're returning from the store and see someone attempting to steal your car. Do you shoot? Or you arrive home and catch a Burglar in the act as they're exiting the back door of your home, with your brand new $3,000 flat screen TV. Do you shoot? While some states do authorize the use of Deadly Physical Force in protecting physical property, it is *HIGHLY* recommended that you do *NOT* use Deadly Physical Force in these situations. While you may be Criminally Justified, it's almost guaranteed you will be hit with a very expensive Wrongful Death Civil suit. Ask yourself; is the property you're attempting to protect worth $2-$3 million, plus attorney's fees?

Now let's say you're returning to your car and witness someone breaking into it, only this time your kids are in the backseat. Or you arrive home to witness someone kicking the door into your house and your family waits inside. Under these circumstances the 'Intent' for why you would choose to use Deadly Physical Force is different because now your intent is to protect 'Life' not property. The use of Deadly Physical Force to prevent Home Invasions and Kidnappings are almost always justified, as long as you're able to effectively accurately articulate the Totality-of-the-Circumstances.

Robberies...

Robberies and burglaries are often misunderstood. A robbery occurs when someone attempts to unlawfully take something of value from another, through the use or threatened use of Physical Force. As mentioned above it is NOT advisable to use Deadly Physical Force to protect your property even if the robber is trying to steal your wallet with $1,000 cash in it. However, robberies automatically introduce one extremely dangerous byproduct. The aggressor IS either using or threatening to use Physical Force and IS typically armed or is giving the impression that they are armed. If you reasonably believe and fear that the threatened Physical Force could actually kill you, then their threated force would give you a reasonable basis for using Deadly Physical Force in return. In this case you're protecting your Life not your property. It's this slight shift of 'Intangible Thought' which makes all the difference. Being proactive and thinking through things today, gives you the ability to present an intellectual basis for your actions tomorrow.

Burglaries...

A burglary occurs when someone unlawfully enters a primes or dwelling with the intent to commit a crime. Typically, a burglar's intent is to steal property similar to that of a robber stealing your wallet. However, now days there's been a recent explosion of Home Invasion Robberies, where the offender's intent is much more than the theft of property.

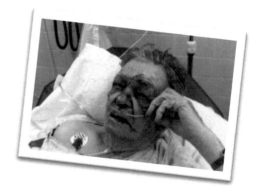

A quick Google search for 'Home Invasion Robberies' will easily give you hundreds of examples of why it's completely reasonable to use Deadly Physical Force to protect against a Home Invasion. But how do you know the assailant's intent is to commit a violent act or just theft? You don't until it's too late. That's where this manual can make all the difference. It provides you an extremely well organized means of retaining actual real-world occurrences, which easily support one's decision to use Deadly Physical Force under those circumstances. The downloading of articles, images and even videos of real-world Home Invasions and other types of Robberies are the kinds of evidence which speak for themselves and can make all the difference in your future Legal Defense. These are the Chess pieces of success you play today, which will quickly and vividly prove the justification of your actions tomorrow.

Being able to present to a Judge and or Jury, an image of the physical injuries sustained by a victim of a Home Invasion Robbery, will stick with that person all the way thorough your trial. Having the ability to reference the random 2007 Cheshire, Connecticut Home Invasion of a family, where a father, his wife and their 11 and 17 year old daughters were beat with baseball bats and bound, where the wife was forced to withdraw $15,000 from her bank and if it couldn't have been worse, the assailants continually beat, raped and tortured the wife and daughters in front of the father over a seven hour period, then torched the house leaving them all to die, this is what compels a third-party to not only see but also feel the degree of fear and anguish that would reasonably lead you to using Deadly Physical Force. In this case the father randomly freed himself but has to live the rest of his days with the vivid memory of his dying wife and kids whom he was hapless to save.

If you are confronted at home, there's no way to know what to expect. In the Cheshire incident, the wife had been dropped off at her bank by one of the suspects. She actually reported the incident to staff who notified police. She described the suspects by their appearance but added that the suspects at this point were "being nice" and suggested she believed they just wanted money. Sadly, the wife exited the bank with the cash and met up with her would be killer before police could arrive.

Think about it, you're typically at your lowest level of awareness when you're at your home. If your door is kicked-in, you usually won't even have adequate time to safely flee, and you're likely accompanied by your family who are also all in immediate danger. Calling 911 only notifies the police that you have a problem. In the Cheshire incident, bank staff notified police who in turn set-up surveillance around the residence, all while this poor family was being raped, tortured and murdered.

Attempting to negotiate, plead for your life, or even trying to go along with the assailant's demands, has time and time again proven NOT to turn out well. But why do authorities advise people to do so, because police don't like vigilantism and all feel that by encouraging potential victims to 'Fight' could bring undue liability on the agency should that person be killed or injured, fighting. It's up to you to determine how to solve that problem until help arrives. Complying with their wishes may work, or it may just seal your fate. If you believe there is a reasonable risk to your life or the lives of your family and you fear that death will result, then it's completely reasonable for you to use Deadly Physical Force to protect said Life. Remember it's about protecting life NOT property.

Criminal vs. Civil Court...

Our Justice System is comprised of two arms, the 'Criminal' and the 'Civil' arms of Justice. While there are some similarities in both, each has their own completely different set of standards and outcomes.

Most people are familiar with the Criminal arm. It's the 'Perry Mason' we grew up watching on TV. While it's entirely possible that you could be arrested even though you're completely innocent, the 'Burden of Proof' for a Criminal conviction is extremely high and referred to as being 'Beyond a Reasonable Doubt.' This basically means the Prosecution must prove that there is 99.9% probability of your guilt and there isn't any rational or logical legally justified reason for why you did what you did. Remember the 'OJ Defense' where OJ Simpson made it appear in Court that his hand did not fit in the glove, which the Prosecution claimed the killer used during the act of murder? Well it worked and the saying stuck, "If it don't fit, you must acquit." All he had to do was present just ONE single form of Reasonable Doubt and he was acquitted of all charges.

Presenting Reasonable Doubt, while also defending against other more damaging concepts of guilt, is not an easy task. In fact, the 'OJ Defense' was a last ditch effort, accompanied by a few other examples of how the Prosecution's case had a few holes. If your Legal Defense strategy is limited to scavenging the Prosecution's evidence, for that single reasonably doubtful element of contradiction, then you have what's called a 'Reactionary Defense'. What I mean by this, is if you haven't already prepared and designed a 'Proactive Legal Defense' such as the one you'll develop with *ZuluShield*, then you're left with a knee-jerk reactionary Defense and are completely limited in your ability to counter a Prosecution's well strategized attack. Basically, you're left 'Waiting' and are stuck playing a game of Poker, hoping that you'll be able to guess the Prosecution's hand and catch them bluffing. But what if they don't bluff, what's your Defense against a solid offence? Utilizing the methods presented in this manual, makes the task of designing the most formidable Defense possible, as easy as 1, 2, 3. It will provide your attorney with a plethora of ready-to-use examples of very strategic Reasonable Doubt solutions, to counter even the most cunning offensive. This way you're not stuck waiting to see if say the Prosecutor's 'Glove' fits or not, like OJ.

The Civil arm of Justice is actually the one which is most likely to ruin you. It's also the one which the vast majority of armed citizens completely misunderstand or even overlook all together. Since It's the comical 'Judge Judy' type proceedings, we view these cases as trivial or some sort of act of comedy. Yet when it comes to a Deadly Force case, a Civil Courtroom is the very last place you'll ever want to find yourself.

You must always remember that just because you've been cleared Criminally, doesn't necessarily mean your legal battle is over. In fact, in any Self-Defense claim; where someone's been seriously injured or killed, if you don't prepare your Defense today, it's not a matter of 'If' you'll be sued but WHEN and how much it's going to cost you. That is unless you properly insulate yourself today. Even if you're found guilty and serving time Criminally, you can still be sued. Talk about a nightmare. The sad reality is that it's not uncommon for every day, legally armed, law abiding citizens to end up in serious trouble Criminally, following the use of Self-Defense. It's also not uncommon for someone to not only lose their home but also end up owing millions of dollars in Civil penalties, even when that use of Self-Defense was found to be 100% justified by both the Police and District Attorneys.

A number of years ago, I learned of a very interesting case of justified Self-Defense and how it turned into a poor victim's nightmare Civilly. The just of the case was that a neurosurgeon started a fight in a bar resulting in the doctor's arrest. The surgeon; who was found to be the 'Aggressor' and eventually found guilty of the assault, successfully sued the victim in Civil Court. During the process of defending themselves, the victim and broke the surgeon's hand resulting in the surgeon being left legally disabled and unable to continue working as a neurosurgeon. Disgustingly, a Civil Court found the victim completely liable and penalized the victim in the sum of $1.5-million.

We hear about these cases all the time and still most people don't think it could ever happen to them. That is until they find themselves in the midst of their very Civil nightmare. The reality is that, if it can happen to 'Them' it can most definitely happen to you. Its up to YOU to protect against it.

 The biggest difference between the two arms of Justice and your greatest threat during any Civil trial, is the Civil System's extremely low Burden of Proof. Civilly, all the Plaintiff has to show is that you 'More Likely Than Not' or by 'Preponderance of The Evidence' violated Civil Law. This is most closely related to a police officer's 'Probably Cause' to arrest. It's an extraordinarily low level of proof, amounting to only 50.01%. Basically, it's just a tip of the scale. During a Wrongful Death suit, such a low burden often proves to be insurmountable. The reason for this is how easy it is for the Plaintiff to bombard the Court with reason after reason for why their loved one should NOT have been killed. Often times all they have to do is come up with just one reasonably sounding argument that their loved one didn't actually pose a serious threat or that you could have just walked away.

Not only is the Burden of Proof extremely low during Civil proceedings, but in many cases the 'Burden' sits on the shoulders of the defendant, which is a stark variance from a Criminal proceeding. You see Criminally, its unto the Prosecution to prove their case. However, in many Civil cases, it's up to you to prove to the Judge or Jury that your actions were Justified. It's this shift of Burden, which is why *ZuluShield* is so extraordinarily vital to your Defense. The only way to prove justification for killing another, is to show example after example of why you simply had to do what you did. It's also vitally important to site actual real-world incidents where other reasonably minded people; who were faced with similar circumstances, chose to take a similar course of action in their own defense. Yet in Court you need 'Proof' not examples by mere testimony. What you'll need are actual print-outs or some form of physical, tactile type evidence which you'll present as an example of 'Reasonable Action' and that's exactly what this system provides. With *ZuluShield*, you'll have a plethora of examples and a multitude of avenues of Defense to justify your actions and prove your innocence.

Let's use a Home Invasion Robbery scenario. We'll say the assailant breaks in your residence in the middle of the night and you're startled from your stupor. You fear for the safety of yourself and your family and decide to arm yourself with your handgun. Knowing police are too far away to intercede, you decide to conduct a Safety Clear of your home. During the process of the clear, you confront the assailant who you find standing 15-feet from you in the middle of your living room. Even though you had expected to find him, you were startled by the sight of him. Your heart's pounding and you soon realize this is the real thing. You can't see his hands and can barely make his face due to the darkness. You notice him begin to walk slowly towards you. Knowing that 'Time' itself is NOT on your side, you decide to shoot and in turn kill him.

Most police investigations would find this to be 'Reasonably Justified Force' due to the fact that the assailant broke in at night, when it's likely you'd be home, thereby posing a greater risk to your safety. Police also know just how quickly a simple Cat Burglary can turn violent. Civilly though, the Assailant's family is going to argue up and down that if you would have only turned on a light, told their loved one to leave or just barricaded your family in the back room, while you waited for police, nobody would have needed to be harmed. Basically the Plaintiff throws spaghetti on the wall till one of their arguments sticks. While you typically can't be imprisoned Civilly, you can most certainly lose everything and never be able to regain your status for the remainder of your life. Scenarios like this one are why this happens. Unless of course you prepare ahead of time.

The 'OJ Defense' does NOT work during a Civil trial. In fact, OJ Simpson ended up being found liable for the Wrongful Death of his ex-wife and was hit with a $25-million penalty. Even though he won his Criminal case, it left him completely bankrupt, so the Civil case hit him even harder leaving him completely insolvent and we all know where that lead him.

Your only hope of avoiding a Civil case is to preemptively gather as much data on Self-Defense cases, brainstorm, then document scenario after scenario of how and why the use of Deadly Physical Force is or has already been found to be Reasonable. The goal is to retain this information and counter each individual argument a Plaintiff could make, with a dozen or more reasons why their argument is NOT reasonable and how Courts have already found your actions to be Justified in similar real-world incidents. *ZuluShield* makes this easy and will be an extraordinarily priceless resource and a vital tool which your attorney can use to unequivocally prove your innocence.

Why a preemptive approach is so vital...

Regardless of whether you find yourself in Criminal or Civil Court, your ability to accurately describe exactly why you chose to do what you did is paramount. It's just as vitally important that you eliminate any chance of misunderstanding whatsoever. It's essential that your reasons for said actions are completely understood so as to be found 'Objectively Reasonable' and not simply Subjective by nature. This requires a degree of articulation that most people simply do not have and that can usually only be accomplished through the assistance of an experienced attorney.

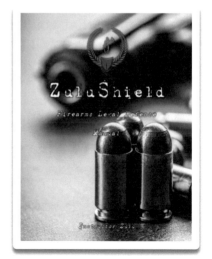

Perspectives of Self-Defense are based on conjuncture. Conjuncture is a kaleidoscope of random yet similar assumptions of an outcome that's based on a thought process of past experiences. Perspectives are also composed of an intangible premonition of impending doom due to exposure of the knowledge of similar previous incidents, all woven together to formulate the facts by which you justified such an extreme action. So, your attorney must fully comprehend the gravity and temperature of your past experiences; whether those experiences actually happened to you or in circumstances where you're basing said actions on a someone else's real-life incident. Then they go about measuring the legality of your actions, so as to determine the best ways to formulate the most accurate explanation to the Court. They do so by selecting the 'Exact' vernacular which BEST describes your Defense.

So how do you do this? How does one explain why they did what they did when you don't even know what particular words best define it? You could wait until you've already acted in Self-Defense. You could attempt at that time and while under the most extreme amounts stress, quickly and off-the-cuff, think back to your past experiences and things you've learned. Then verbally describe those concepts to your attorney, while drawing context to the incident in question. This is what most people do but it's far from the most accurate. Sure you may remember particular things of importance, but having the ability to combine it all together so it's presentable and palatable in Court, is an entirely different story all together.

What this system provides is a means of preemptively communicating these facts to your attorney, to afford you the BEST chances of obtaining the most solid legal advice and services, customized to your particular individual needs, without being required to actively think back and remember things from say five, ten or even twenty years in the past. This manual is also specifically designed to give you the most practical means of retaining important data of similar incidents that happened to someone else, which may later actually play an active role in your decision process. *ZuluShield* also provides a similar way of retaining these incidents of Self-Defense, which Courts have previously found to be reasonable. This way you don't have to remember minute facts, times, places or even people involved, all those years later while under enormous stress. All you have to do is flip through your convenient and strategically structured *ZuluShield Archive*.

Let's revisit the Home Invasion Robbery scenario from earlier. Remember the assailant breaks in your residence in the middle of the night and you're startled from your stupor. You decide to grab your firearm and clear your house, when you confront the assailant who's standing in your living room. You're scared and can't see if he's armed or not, decide to shoot and in turn kill him. You determined your course of action for a number of reasons:

1. The person unlawfully entered and is remaining in your home.

2. Its night so you conclude that he must have assumed you'd be home, which means he would have reasonably planned for you being there and although you can't see a weapon, you believe it reasonable under those circumstances that he would have armed himself.

3. You also decided to shoot based on the fact that you know Home Invasion Robberies to be extremely dangerous and unpredictable.

4. You chose NOT to warn or tell the intruder to 'Freeze' because you know from training that 'Action' is always faster than 'Reaction' and you FEARED that by giving the intruder any more time to contemplate an attack, WOULD cost you your life.

5. Now let's say you've come to this conclusion because of a number of incidents in the past which you've seen or read about in the News and one in particular stood out, which you end up specifically siting.

All of this is mixed together and clearly articulates a reasonable basis for your actions and that you reasonably feared that your life and your family's were in grave danger and you were justified in the use of Deadly Physical Force to protect 'Life'. In no time, you're able to give clear articulation supported by tangible facts. Now contrast that with a 'Reactive Defense Strategy' where you're left picking up the pieces while you develop your Defense on-the-fly.

"That's good!" you say, "that's what I want!" Yes, the above mentioned rundown of articulation is wonderful and will undoubtedly keep you out of jail. However, for Court purposes you need much, much more. You need hard facts, something tangible, otherwise its mere conjecture and is far too 'Subjective' by nature. In Court you must present factual detail. The Court needs to know the dates and times of those past incidents you've eluded to as part of your decision process for using force. You must also show why any of that actually relates to the context of your particular Self-Defense claim. Trying to remember all this information and the overwhelming amount of other important facts, all while under the gauntlet of extreme stress, is an uphill battle and the reason why so many people fail so miserably in Court and exactly why they either plead or settle Civilly despite their innocence.

ZuluShield is specifically designed to make your Court proceedings a much easier and more successful experience. With this system you'll not only learn how to effectively articulate example after example, but your attorney will have those examples right there at their fingertips, all strategically organized to give you a bulletproof Legal Defense. Your due diligence today, will pay dividends tomorrow.

A proactive approach to tomorrow's legal battle is your only hope for success. Learn why *ZuluShield* is Firearms Legal Defense made easy. Discover the secrets you need to know today to protect against future legal action. Turn to Page 133 to learn how you can start protecting yourself today.

4
Concealed Carry

The subject of Concealed Carry is rive with controversy. We're currently experiencing the largest spike in Concealed Handgun License (CHL) applicants in history. For some it's a rite of passage, for others it's as evil as Sin itself. The fact still remains, Concealed Carry is here and it's not going away. In fact, recent U.S. Supreme Court decisions have opened the floodgates. The days of Firearms Prohibition by municipalities like Chicago and D.C. are gone. The masses are beginning to figure out that the best solution to a deadly threat, is the preparedness of an armed citizen. With the increase of outlandish acts of horror, citizens far and wide have finally understood just how important it is that they be ready and able to stand in their own defense.

Interesting enough, the largest spike in CHL applications are amongst females and Democrats; who have historically pushed Gun Control and Restriction. Yet even they can't ignore the explosion of random crime, which plagues our urban centers and threatens to rewrite the fabric of sleepy suburbia. When people who previously supported Gun Control are not only advocating gun ownership but rather day to day carry, you know something's afoot. Throngs of people have lost hope in our public safety professionals and have decided to take proactive steps to protect their own lives. As opposed to be killed armed only with a phone, as they dial 911 to notify Police about where to bring the Medical Examiner, they've gone about arming themselves with firearms, for the probability of tomorrow's attack.

Why should you carry?

As mentioned previously, random crime is on the rise. Violent robberies, assaults, rapes and home invasions have become an epidemic. Add to this the spike in Active Shooter/Active Threat type incidents and you soon realize that your vulnerability is real and you can be attacked anywhere at any time. When Chiefs of Police and Sheriffs across America, urge their citizens to get armed, you know there's a problem. When professionals; who's sworn duty is to 'Protect' their communities, one by one tell their citizenry that law enforcement is incapable of protecting them, you know there's an epidemic. However, choosing to arm one's self and carry their weapon concealed should NEVER be taken lightly. There are a few very important factors to consider prior to entertaining such an idea. Facing this dilemma during a real-life fight for your life, only makes you more vulnerable and less capable at thwarting such an attack.

While the 2nd Amendment of the United States Constitution affirms the individual citizen a right to be armed, it doesn't mean you should just run off to buy any ol firesitck. You have a responsibility as a citizen to be armed and ready, but you also share in the responsibility of maintaining safe and prudent ownership. The following are 10 important questions you should answer BEFORE you ever don a handgun for daily protection.

1. Are you mentally prepared to carry?

The number one most overlooked aspect of Self-Defense; especially as it relates to firearms, is the psychological framework of the defender. Most people rightly assume there's a psychological factor, however they fail to properly think 'Through' the gravity of such an occurrence. The result is usually one of two outcomes. The ill prepared defender will either under-react or over-react, thereby exponentially exposing themselves to death or imprisonment. All this for trying to do the 'Right' thing. Here are four important questions you should consider:

I. **Why am I choosing to carry?:** Its important to determine exactly why you believe it's necessary to be armed. Carrying a firearm is never something to take lightly. Sure it sounds cool and is usually associated with a sense of 'Power'. However, with that power comes an enormous amount of both liability and responsibility. Your reasoning should never come from a 'Just Because' type approach. Instead your rational should be rooted in the mindset of 'Preparedness'. It should be because you wholeheartedly believe and are fully convinced, that there exists a high probability that you'll be forced in a situation, where your life or the life of another will be threatened. Your reasoning should be founded on the concept that you accept the liability and take on the responsibility'for defending life and will do everything within your power to assure that you're prepared both physical and mentally for such an occurrence.

II. **Am I mature and responsible enough to carry?:** Maturity is NOT something which comes with age. It's a bit like 'Common Sense', its really not that common at all. Carrying a firearm requires an extreme amount of maturity, it requires someone to first 'Know' their responsibilities and then 'Own' them. You MUST be a person who's able to compose themselves in stressful situations, especially when offended or angered. There is NO room for poor judgment or a hot temper while armed. While the 2nd Amendment may grant every citizen the right to carry. However, most lack the character and judgment of a responsible person and with all honesty, should NOT carry. Be honest with yourself, if you're not ready to bear the weight of responsibility, you're NOT ready to bear arms.

III. **Am I emotionally and psychologically stable enough to carry?:** Here's another largely overlooked reality of responsible gun ownership. The question of being emotionally and psychologically sound is NOT one purely posed to those who suffer from mental health issues. It's actually a gut-check to us all. At some point and really at many points throughout our lives, otherwise 'Healthy Minded' persons WILL experience emotional and psychological lows. Its vitally important to understand that you must be a person who's aware of his or herself. You need to be in-tune with your emotional cycle. It's also critical that you're a person who can generally control your emotions. Everybody loses their temper, its part of life, but if you're carrying a weapon, there is NO room for a hot temper. On the flip side, there is also ZERO room for cowardice while armed. A hot temper will land you in prison and cowardice will likely cause your untimely death. Its also highly probable, that if you cower in the face of attack, your weapon will be taken and used, not just against you but another persons. You must be someone of SOUND mind. For those who suffer from major mental health issues, you should completely abstain from owing weapons altogether. For those who consider themselves 'Healthy Minded', you will experience lows. Its important to understand that during those lows, you should consider locking your guns away until the storm blows over.

Second to gang violence, domestic disputes and altercations amongst family and friends, make up the bulk of firearms related homicieds. What many fail to realize, is that most of these individuals are NOT psycopaths. They are everyday 'Normal' people, who had a VERY bad day. What happens is they simply fail to stay aware of their emotional state. They spiral out of control and their impulses take the better of them. Knowing ahead of time, that you're one bad day from a VERY bad day, will help you stay ahead of the curve. You'll grasp the important balancing act of remaining responsible even during times of extreme emotional hardship.

2. **How will this affect my current lifestyle?** Think about it, you're planning on carrying a weapon 24-7. So what does that mean? It means, everywhere you go you must be on your 'A-Game'. Your behavior must always be tip top and your tactical readiness and awareness must always be on point. There's simply no room for errors of judgment and conduct while armed. On top of always being on your best behavior, everything else changes. In reality, your lifestyle must revolve around you being armed. It must be a focal point not an afterthought. Anywhere and everywhere you go, you'll need to consider how you and your firearm fit into the equation. It's a constant mathematical equation. There are places you simply won't be allowed and you'll need to know those places ahead of time. One of the biggest

frustrations for most Concealed Carriers are security check points. Obviously you're not gonna attempt to board a plane while armed. However, there are an increasing number of metal detectors and scrutinized security at ball games, event centers and even malls. Being armed means you'll have to plan for contingencies should you happen upon a place that doesn't allow firearms. Your wardrobe will also change especially if you're carrying on your person, which is exactly how you should. Simple things like how you walk and carry yourself, all this will change too. Why, because the last thing you wanna do is walk or stand in a manner that tells the whole world you've got a gun under your shirt. If you're into hiking, jogging or live an active life, you'll need to consider what to do with your firearm during those activates. How about work? Are you allowed to carry at work? You should scrutinize your entire lifestyle today, so you know ahead of time what needs tweaking.

3. Are your family and close friends aware?

Something you likely haven't considered is how your decision to carry effects those closest to you. Its vitally important that you spend some time today to brainstorm those effects. This is especially true when considering how this impacts those actually living with you. It is strongly suggested that everyone who lives with you, undergoes a handgun safety class. You should also have a safety plan. Family members must know what to do should you become incapacitated or they happen upon an unsecure firearm in the home. This type of education is even more important if you have young children in the home. With the increase in firearms ownership, has come an increase in completely preventable and tragic firearms catastrophes in the home. This typically involves young children who've happened upon an unsecure loaded weapon. You MUST be prepared beforehand and know how to properly introduce and infuse your firearm in to their daily lives. This is also true for close friends. Let's say you're out on the town with them and have a medical emergency. What are you going to do with your firearm? Who's going to secure it while you're rushed to the hospital? How about if you're incapacitated while you're attempting to defend yourself or another? Will your friends know what to do? You may also have friends and family who are 100% anti-gun and will under no circumstances, allow you in their homes while you're armed. It's vital that you come to grips with the fact that, your decision to carry will directly affect those closet to you. Making them aware and equipping them with the knowledge of how to be safe, is essential and it's your responsibility.

4. Where and when will you carry?

Have you already determined when you'll carry? Are you planning on carrying everywhere you go 24-7, or are you just wanting to be armed on specific occasions? It's extremely important that you think this through now. We just touched on this, if you're going to carry 24-7, you've got to take into account the places you simply WON'T be allowed to. We've also discussed a few effects on your lifestyle should you choose to carry in public. These are considerations you must plan for today. For instance, I know a lady who works as a Legal Assistant. She works and lives in a more dangerous area of town. Her decision to carry; like most, was based on Self-Protection, because she lives and works in a violent world. However, her job also has her going in and out of courthouses all day long. She had to consider beforehand, how she'd secure her weapon while at work during court visits.

Some employers won't allow you to carry. Does yours? What are you going to do if they don't? Breaking 'Employee Policy' can get you fired, but what about the Law and those places that are against the Law to carry? All too often otherwise law abiding citizens find themselves in a world of hurt, when they inadvertently get caught carrying a firearm in a place where they're forbidden by Law to carry. When it comes to the Law, 'Ignorance' is NOT a defense. Just because you didn't 'Know' you weren't allowed to carry in a particular place, won't matter. Breaking firearms laws have devastating lifelong consequences. You will be charged with a Felony and you will also lose your right to carry and even own firearms altogether. You think it's hard to find a job now, imagine trying to find one after being charged with a gun crime. Do you know where you're forbidden by Law to carry? You need to.

- Post Offices
- State & Federal Buildings
- Most State & Federal Lands (this includes forests)
- Some Police Stations
- Schools
- Some Private Venues (Casinos, Sports Arenas, Concert Halls)

These are but a few common places you're bound to visit in your lifetime. If you're planning on carrying 24-7, you'll need to determine where and how you'll go about securing your weapon before you set foot in or on one of these premises.

Let's say you simply what to carry on special occasions or just in the car. How are you going to secure your weapon when it's not in your direct control? The benefit to 24-7 carry, is that you'll quickly become accustomed to carrying and will hopefully form a habit of safety. The down side to occasional carry, is the potential that carrying becomes an afterthought and safety goes out the window. Where and When you carry will also directly affect the type of firearm you should carry. If you're planning on carrying at work but where a business suite all day, then you might just need to consider carrying a sub-compact handgun during at work then switch back to a more standard concealable size when you're not at work. There are many, many factors to consider when it relates to When and Where you'll carry. Take the time now to brainstorm how your choice to carry will impact your daily life.

5. How will you carry?

There's a plethora of carry options available, from holsters, pouches, purses and packs, the list could go on and on. People carry on their waist, in their pockets, on their ankles and even in their bras. Determining ahead of time exactly how you'll carry, will help you avoid tomorrow's headache. Like most people, you'll likely find out you're in for a wardrobe change.

Don't take this lightly it's very important that you think about all the factors ahead of time. Determining if it's the right fit for the job, is a vital step in Concealed Carry. Planning ahead of time will also assure that you maintain safety. One of the top reasons for Negligent Discharges have to do with improper or unsatisfactory holster set-ups. Do your homework, just because it's popular doesn't mean it's safe and if you saw it in the movies, it's almost a guaranteed No Go.

Keep in mind, purses, bags and pouches are convenient, but they do pose a safety hazard especially when left unattended. A recent case in a super market, involved a lady's toddler who grabbed her handgun from her purse, while he sat in the grocery cart. He then fatally shot her while they stood in the checkout line. A well-known firearms advocate was recently shot by her young child who found a firearm on the floorboard of the car. Thankfully she survived, but now she faces serious criminal consequences and could actually loser custody of her child. There was another case were a lady accidently shot and killed herself while adjusting her bra gun in a store. There are countless cases of guys shooting themselves in their crotch because they've carried their firearms in their pants without a holster. Or how about NFL'er Plaxico Burress who shot himself in the leg while he danced in a club wearing sweatpants. And what about all those guns that go sliding across the the busy sidewalk when thy fall from ankle holsters. Happens all the time but people see ankle holsters on TV and actually think they work. Be wise my friends, negligence is a crime.

The safest, most secure and practical place to carry is on your hip. This can be achieved with an Outside-The-Waistband or Inside-The-Waistband rig. While this is the best way to carry, it might not work for you and your circumstances. For instance, ladies find it especially difficult in locating the right match of holster and clothing for on the hip carry. If you can't carry on your waist, determine the next best option for you and invest in a <u>QUALITY</u> holster or concealment system, going cheap will exponentially work against you.

6. How will you secure your weapon?

Here's another area for contention. I've heard people argue up and down that it's their right as American's NOT to secure their weapons. While I agree, it doesn't mean we shouldn't secure them. The reality is that someone is going to get a hold of your otherwise unsecure weapon when you're not looking and that someone is either going to shoot someone else or themselves and YOU will be the one the Police come looking for. Even if you don't get charged with a crime, you WILL be sued and you had better expect to payout millions to the deceits' family.

You've probably heard it said that Gun Control means using both hands. Unless your weapon is in your hands or on your person, you had better determine how you're going to secure it. There's plenty of options available, some better than others. Regardless of your choice, be sure you NEVER leave your weapon unattended without first securing it under lock and key.

7. Do you have the training?

Firearms training is vital. However, as previously mentioned, having the 'Right' training is crucial. Your commitment to training should be considered 'Lifelong'. You must also grasp the costs associated with this training and that you'll be require to set aside time on a regular basis to polish-up and perfect your craft.

Your gun is not always going to be the best solution. The real weapon is your mind and how you use it. For that reason, you must prepare your mind and commit to learning other forms of Self-Defense, such as Krav Maga. Even in circumstances where using a gun is justified, many people have found that the totality of the circumstances at hand and the close proximity to their Threat, impedes their ability to even access their gun. You must know how to use your mind in a fight to determine the best solution.

You'll also need to understand you will never learn everything. There are multiple ways to skin a cat as they say, so keep an open mind. What you're looking for are Fighting Skills, not Shooting Skills. You need tactics that work in the real-world. In this day and age, everybody claims to be an expert instructor. There's also an enormous number of returning Vet's or shall I say self-proclaimed Vet's claiming to be Special Forces Gurus. Sadly, many commit Stolen Valor, are complete fakes. Likewise, most instructors have NEVER even been in a gunfight much less served on an SOF team or ever had to use the tactics they're promoting. Its' not important that they've fought in a war or served on an Alpha Team. What is important is the authenticity of their experience. It's also important to understand that simply being a decorated Navy SEAL, doesn't mean they're a good instructor. Teaching is a skill just like fighting. Find quality instructors who know what they're talking about and who actually 'Teach' practical fighting skills, NOT competitive race-gun shooting.

Remember Chapter (1), the elements to 'Sound Combatives Training':

1. Firearms Kata
2. Stress Inoculation
3. Tactical Training

Take your training serious. You're not training for a completion, you're training for War. You need all (3) components for a sure victory. Seek quality professional training and always, always, always remember to perfect your Kata. Turn to Page 130 to learn how *ZuluFight* will help achieve that.

8. Do you know the law?

Hands down the #1 most overlooked aspect of any Self-Defense incident is what happens 'After'. Too often people assume they'll respond reasonably when attacked and fail to take the much needed time today, to think 'Through' such a chaotic set of circumstances. Knowing what you can and can't do, as well as what you should or shouldn't do, are critical. Yes, there is a stark difference between 'Can' and 'Should'. When it comes to Self-Defense, there are many times when you may be justified in a particular course of action, yet given the totality of the circumstances, you really shouldn't use that specific response. Instead, you may just find that you should respond in a much different manner. Understanding how and when to make these calculations is the difference between winning both the battle and the war. Too often everyday legally armed citizens, find themselves on the wrong end of the Law and or Civil lawsuits, simply because they lack the wisdom gained from a proactive approach to tomorrow's legal battle.

In Chapter (3) we discussed just how vague Self-Defense Laws actually are. You <u>NEED</u> to know your State's Self-Defense laws in and out. However, simply knowing the Law isn't good enough. You must also have a proactive legal defense plan, specifically designed to give you the most favorable outcome 'After' your future use of Self-Defense. That legal defense plan should start today, while you have the time to research, gather and be strategic in your preparation. As we've discussed, simply being 'Justified' in defending yourself, won't protect you against a devastating Civil lawsuit. The valuable resource you'll find from *ZuluShield*, will prove to be immeasurably beneficial when your use of Self-Defense is scrutinized. Take the time today and invest in a system that does the hard work for you. Find out how *ZuluShield* can protect you from devastating a legal melee on Page 133.

9. Do you have a Self-Defense Plan?

It's been said that "No battle plan survives first contact." Due to the chaotic influences of completely uncontrollably random circumstances present in EVERY fight, it's impossible to predict the outcomes of battle. If you're like most people, you likely haven't developed a "What will I do when I'm attacked" approach to tomorrow's deadly threat. Instead, you're probably either tabling it for later, or have a "I'll cross that bridge when I get there" attitude. Even though you can't predict outcomes, the worst thing you could ever do, is show up to a gunfight without a gun. Showing up without a 'Plan', well that's like having a gun with no ammunition.

You need to have a plan and that plan begins with a 'What When Mentality'. The best approach to the unknown, is to make it more 'Known'. You do this by brainstorming as many different possible scenarios in which you'll be faced with the decision to use Self-Defense. For each 'When' scenario, you need to take the time to formulate at least (3) different ways of overcoming such an occurrence. Without this depth of forethought, your response tomorrow; to a completely random chaotic event, will be a randomly chaotic reaction based solely on 'Chance'. Battle planing today gives you a preview of things to come. Doing so means you're able to make 'Rational' decisions today completely abcent the immedate and overwelming chaos of tomorrow. Best of all you encode numerous future on-the-spot decisions; each with multiple different solutions, so no matter the spacific and unique circumstances, you're afforded the most educated responses.

10. What firearm will you carry?

The last thing you'll want to do is show up to a gun shop and expect a salesperson; who's job it is to make a profit, know what handgun is best for you and then offer the best price for that gun. Just because someone sells guns, doesn't mean they have any clue whatsoever about what handguns are best in an actual fight. It also doesn't mean they even know anything about guns in general other than which ones are more popular. But how does one determine which one is best, especially if the person purchasing is a novice and has never held a handgun, much less shot one before? Well you're going to have to do some research and figure this one out BEFORE your trip to the gun store. What you'll need to do is base that decision on the mission. Brining the wrong tool to a gunfight is like trying to use a hammer to turn a screw. I guess it can be done, but it's going to take a whole lot of time and effort. If the mission requires a small gun, why buy a big one? And if Murphy's Law decides to pay a visit, wouldn't you want the most reliable option available? I've dedicated a whole section in Chapter (5) on this subject. I'll point out my Top 3 choices for Personal Defense in Full-Size, Compact and Sub-Compact. I'll also cover ammunition types, which work best in actual gunfights.

11. Can you actually kill someone?

When it relates to the topic of Concealed Carry, I've saved this all important question for last. I did this, to leave a very REAL, sobering and bitter taste in your mouth. If your answer is anything but a resounding YES! then you have no business whatsoever carrying a firearm. Don't get me wrong, I'm not suggesting that 'Yes' should be based on a gleeful anticipation of brining death to another. What I am asserting, is that your answer should be so unequivocally certain, that there is no hesitation or even an inkling of doubt or remorse. When that day comes, there should be NO remorse for choosing to live or protect the existence of another, as opposed to succumbing to or turning your eyes as another person suffers an untimely violent end.

Firearms are tools of death; they are devices which aid in the act of killing. Carrying a handgun for Concealed Carry purposes, means you anticipate a likelihood, that one day you WILL be thrust into the grips of Death itself. Because of the high probability of such a circumstance, you've decided to preemptively hedge against its outcome by concealing a 'Secret Weapon', which you'll use to snatch your life back and live to tell about that experience.

The act of killing is a topic you MUST take the time today to completely digest, so when tomorrow comes and a demon stands before you, you'll act without hesitation or remorse. The best way to begin this journey of conceptual preparation, is to think about your most loved family member or friend, someone you simply can't go without. For instance, this could be your newborn baby. Now imagine a man with a knife to your baby's throat. You know for certain that this man will force the knife deep into your baby's neck and your baby will be brutally murdered before you. You can hear the frantic screams of your baby now, as the man holds them with a grip that's already likely broken their shoulder. You hear those cries and know, the pain they feel now, will be nothing like the pain they will feel seconds from now, when that man forces his knife into their neck. In your hand is a loaded handgun and you have a choice. You can save your baby's life or you can hopelessly allow them to die a most painful death. Your firearm is a tool; it cannot act or think for itself. It's up to you to employ that weapon and use it in the manner in which it was created to be used.

What When? Would you feel remorseful for saving your baby's life? Would you hesitate or would you immediately act and kill that man, before your baby experiences the worst kind of pain and is taken forever? What <u>WILL</u> you do?

If this scenario and the depth of its description has shocked you, if it offended you to the very marrow of your bones, good. Death and killing are the most extreme experiences you'll ever know. Carrying a firearm as a means of killing; so as to prevent death, is the second most extreme thing you'll ever do in life. Using your hands to kill another is <u>THE</u> most extreme thing you'll ever do. In order to ready yourself you must take time to completely submerge yourself in the sickening conceptual role-play of the actual act of killing. You need to think with such focus and description, that you become sick to your stomach. Only then will you arrive at your unequivocal solution for the most disgusting and offensive circumstance you'll ever know. If, however you're unable to stomach a mental journey to the valley called Death. If you can't even think about the possibility of a circumstance of such extremes, then please whatever you do, <u>DON'T</u> purchase or even carry a firearm.

5
Zulu's Top Picks

You've decided to arm yourself to hedge against an attack on your existence. You don't know when or where this attack may occur, but you've decided to be ready. Do you have the 'Best' tool for the job? Is there even a such thing as the best firearm, or does it come down to personal preference?

I'm going to argue that there is a best choice for Personal Defense. There is a plethora of choices out there, many are completely impractical, while some are okay and a few are decent and should get the job done. However, there are a specific breed of handgun, which are inherently better suited for Personal Defense, no matter the circumstance or environment. This chapter is focused on giving you my Top 3 Full-Size, Concealed Carry and Sub-Compact handguns as well as the best caliber and ammunition choices.

The right choice...

There are thousands of different types of handguns from hundreds of different manufactures, but not all handguns are created equal. When determining the right handgun for Personal Defense, there are a few key factors to keep in mind:

1. **Suited:** The reason you're even acquiring a weapon is to 'Defend Life'. It's NOT for looks, plinking at the range or for competition. It's for the sole purpose of Self-Defense. What it boils down to, is you require a Combat Handgun. You need something specifically suited for gunfights not a show gun. The handgun itself must by nature be:

   - Practical
   - Reliable
   - Simplistic

It's important your handgun's inherent qualities are practical and afford ease of use under varying circumstances. For instance, one overlooked reality of Firearms Self-

Defense, relates to the fluidity of movement during the fight. The veracity of this movement has a direct effect on the functionality of any given handgun. One of the most common handgun failures is the Type 2 Malfunction and pertains 'Yaw Effect. This is where the handgun is exposed to twisting or an oscillation of movement off its vertical axis, while in the process of shooting or recoil. Basically gravity acts against recoil and the firearm fails to fully eject its spent casing. If there's one thing you can be certain of, it's that your fight WILL be dynamic and be subject to continual movement with a constantly changing shooting platform. So when it comes to practicality you'll want to make sure you choose a handgun that will perform well despite the veracity by which you fight.

Good Ol Murphy loves to pop his head up when we can least afford it. You can bet he'll be there during your fight. For this reason, it's critical that you choose the most reliable option out there. You need a handgun that will work no matter what, regardless of the abuse. While all Combat Handguns are suited for a fight, some are far more dependable for ANY fight regardless of when and where. You'll need to realize that you'll likely be carrying your handgun on a daily basis. Because of this your gun will be exposed to things like, lint and dust, as well as many other substances. Your handgun will also experience the extreme changes of temperature and humidity as you regularly go from the comfortable conditions of your home, car or office, to the extremes of the outdoors. All of these factors directly affect your handgun's functionality. Some Handguns require far more maintenance than others, simply to keep them functional. Some handguns are specifically designed to function even under the worst conditions, without regular maintenance. You need a Timex, a handgun that takes a lickin but keeps on tickin.

The most frustratingly consistent reality about almost every incident of Self-Defense, relates to the fact that 'Action' is always faster than 'Reaction', and you're almost always 'Reacting' to a deadly threat. Time is NOT on your side. In Chapter (2) we learned that when reacting to a shooting Threat, you could easily be shot 6-10 times before you're even capable of shooting back. Is there any sense in adding more reaction time by choosing to fight with a weapon that's harder to use and requires multiple manipulations, just to get it to shoot? Simplicity is key! Your handgun's functionality should adhere to the Keep It Simple Stupid (KISS) methodology. It should be streamlined, free from unneeded accessories, capable of ambidextrous shooting and more of a 'Point and Shoot' gun as opposed to one that requires the manipulation of safeties and other buttons. When the shit hits the fan and your life is determined by the speed and violence of your fight, you're NOT gonna want a $600-$700, 3lb paperweight that you can't get off 'Safe'. KISS, it works every time.

2. **Tailored:** All Combat Handguns are suited for the task of fighting and all will get the job done, however which one is 'Best' for you comes down to your mission. If you knew the time and place of attack, then you'd bring a rifle and about 10 friends with rifles, but you don't and you can't. So your objectives for Personal Defense pertain mainly to proactive daily preparation or Concealed Carry / Home Defense. There are (3) types of Combat Handguns:

    - Full-Size
    - Compact / Concealed Carry
    - Sub-Compact / Pocket Carry

It's best to select a handgun that's suited for the particular task at hand. If you're defending your home, a Full-Size handgun is 'Best' suited. So tailoring your Home Defense gun to a Full-Size variant would be best. If it Summer time and you've decided to head out on the town, a Full-Size gun would probably be completely impractical, since you'll likely be wearing shorts and a t-shirt. So in this case, you may need to resort to a Sub-Compact variant. Even though the Sub-Compact variant is say 'Three Stars' to the Full-Size's 'Five Stars', your mission dictates your equipment, so choose the best Sub-Compact option available. Your mid-sized or compact options are a great alternative because they offer the best of both worlds. There may even be occasions when you'll need an extremely small gun, which fits in your pocket. Whatever your choice is just remember to tailor the handgun to your mission and purchase a handgun that scores high in Practicality, Reliability and Simplicity.

Which gun is best?

This is by far the biggest controversy amongst firearms owners in forever. I'll admit there might not be a Holy Grail of Combat Handguns, but most handguns are not a viable option for an actual gunfight. They're just not suited for the task. Since your fight will ultimately be based on you attempting to protect your life, wouldn't it be wise to show up to that fight with the very best weapon capable of helping you win that fight? However, if you're not a tactical professional, how do you go about finding out which handguns to avoid? You accomplish this by learning what's most important in a gunfight. You weed-out the guns that won't work by prioritizing what's most important in a gunfight. Which is, multiple rounds on Threat, in the shortest of time spans, regardless of the circumstances, all the time, every time. I'm going to show you my Top 3 picks but it's up to you to decide what makes the most sense.

We just discussed the importance of going with a weapon that's both Suits and is Tailored to the fight. As we discussed, a Combat or Tactical Handgun, is specifically designed for a gunfight. Most Combat Handguns will get the job done, however there is one that stands out as the most practical, dependable and reliable handgun for tactical purposes. It's also one hated by many. Why, because most people simply don't understand Combat itself or the power of 'Simplicity' as a defense. The more complicated something is, the more likely it is to fail, especially under stress. As you've learning in Chapter (2), there's no place more stress ridden than the middle of a fight for your life.

Since the Flintlock, the Revolver style handgun is 1st Generation handgun technology. There is a reason why the Revolver was replaced in battle. While they are compact and pretty easy to use, they do not provide the tactical advancements of a decent semi-auto. Hence they are NOT suited for a fight. Due to a complete lack of fighting experience by the vast majority of firearms enthusiasts, the Revolver is still the go to Concealed Carry firearm for many an armed citizen.

One of the main proponents to why people inadvertently show-up to a gunfight with inferior weapons, goes all the way back to the purchase of those weapons. Unfortunately, many gun store clerks push the Revolver because of their simplicity. However, simplicity itself is NOT the only factor which makes-up a solid Combat Handgun. Revolver have three huge setbacks. They simply don't hold enough rounds, are horribly difficult to reload under pressure and lack the ergonomics of modern day handguns. Gun dealers ignore these truths. Instead they believe new shooters; especially ladies, don't have the ability to carry semi-autos. What's crazy is that if given a choice between the two, that same clerk would take a semi-auto over even the most well-made Revolver. Remember, your whole reason for owning a handgun, is because you believe that someday you'll need to use it to protect your life or someone else's. You need to show-up to that fight with the best tool suited and tailored for that fight.

In the 1890's a tactical genius by the name of John M. Browning, took it upon himself to devise a more practical Combat Handgun to replace Samuel Colt's 1830's Revolver. The Revolver was outdated and had become a hindrance in battle. What was needed was a more ergonomically correct, semi-automatic, which could be more easily reloaded on the move and could hold more rounds. They also needed a weapon which was capable of withstanding the abuse of battle as well as its exposure to sand, dirt and weather. Browning's new design literally changed the face of battle and has proved to be just as revolutionary as his machine gun advancements.

In fact, the M1911 Pistol went on to be the longest serving firearm in American History. For 100 years its stood as the Gold Standard of modern Combat Handguns. Like a number of tried and tested weapons of its era, the 1911 Pistol is still as lethal today as it was in the 1890's. However, like anything, times change and so does technology.

Think about the aerospace industry and its role in modern warfare. In the very same year that the 1911 Pistol was introduced to the battlefield, so to was the single-seat prop engine 1911 Deperdussin Monoplane. Most people wouldn't even know it, but if it hadn't been for this now archaic monoplane, we wouldn't have the F-22 Raptor, F-16 Fighting Falcon or any of our modern attack fighters. Could you imagine though, showing up to a Dog Fight next week flying a Monoplane?

The 1911 Pistol is a fine weapon but its old 2nd Generation technology, going on 126 years and counting. In that span of time, things have changed and weaponry has evolved into a much more efficient and practical design.

In 1982 another tactical genius Austrian born; Gaston Glock, took the semi-auto pistol to a whole new world. Since then, the Glock 17 went Platinum and has set a whole new standard in modern day weaponry. The Glock is by far the most straight forward Combat Handgun in existence. It's also the easiest semi-auto handgun to operate by novice and experts, men and women, big or small. It's truly the closet thing you'll get to a 'Point and Shoot' weapon.

It's specifically designed to adhere to the KISS methodology and is probably the main reason many of its decenters have issue with it. Most notably the Glock does not have a dedicated safety. Why, because the only safety a Combat Handgun should have, is the acuitive judgment of the person who's employing the weapon itself. If you think back to the torrent of outside stressors that you'll face when you're attacked and the realities of Action vs. Reaction discussed in Chapter (2), you'll quickly understand why taking extra time to manipulate a safety, would NOT be ideal during a gunfight.

Some would argue that with practice, it takes no time at all to teach one's self to manipulate a safety during a gunfight. I would argue wholeheartedly against that. I've been in numerous incidents where very well trained individuals have forgotten to disengage their safeties in a fight and been left pulling on a trigger that even the Hulk couldn't make work. Ask around and you'll find this to be a very common and deadly reality. The reason is that when those individuals saw a Threat to their existence and their minds conceived a way to fight that Threat, the only thing their fingers remembered was to depress the trigger. Due to the stress, they forgot about the safety. Yet let's say you are able to disengage the safety, it will still take around a quarter second. Again if you remember about Reaction Times in Chapter (2), you'll know that in that quarter second, the Treat could easily send (1) round your direct. What if that round hits you in your face? That doesn't sound offal 'Safe' to me. Even if your Threat misses, how much time do really wanna waste fumbling around pushing buttons or flipping switches? The reality is that in a gunfight, when you're acting in Self-Defense, time is NOT on your side and you'll want a weapon that's simple and effective.

Others would argue that a Glock is not as accurate as say a Wilson Combat 1911. Well that may be true, but the variance of accuracy between an out of the box $450 Glock, compared to a $5,000 Wilson, only amounts to about quarter inch at best. When it comes to handgun battles and handgun distances, that quarter inch is meaningless, especially when you take into account the practical advantages the Glock affords over the 1911.

A Glock is far more agronomical for nearly everyone, making it both easier to manipulate and shoot. It's also much lighter than a 1911. This too is an area of argument, because some refer to the Glock as a 'Plastic Gun'. However, if I can drive a dump truck over my Glock, retrieve it, depress the trigger and know without a shadow of a doubt, that it will operate flawlessly, then I'm not so worried about it's so called 'Plastic' frame. In fact, the Polymer 2 frame is scientifically more resilient than carbon steel and most other steel alloy guns, to include the 1911. That's scientific fact. Think about it, Polymer 2 is what you call a 'Technology Advancement' kinda like Titanium is to the aerospace industry. Polymer 2 costs less to produce, meaning you pay less and it weighs less than a steel framed gun. That's a win in my book all day long. The Glock also has far fewer parts than all of its competition. Less parts means an exponential decrease in potential malfunctions, making it an inherently more dependable system altogether. Another advantage to a less moving parts, means the Glock is extremely easy to clean and maintain.

Glocks also boast of Double Stack Magazines, while 1911's only has Single Stacks. It's always better to have more and not need than to need it and not have enough. A Glock 17 affords you (18) ways to kill your Threat, while a standard 1911 only gives you (8). On top of all this, the Glock is the Timex that takes a lickin and keeps on tickin. You can abuse the Glock and expose it to the worst imaginable conditions and it will function as it did the first day you took it out of its box. One of my Glocks has hundreds of thousands of rounds through it and I've never had to replace a thing, not even a spring. I've been around firearms for years and years and there's simply no other handgun with such a degree of consistent dependability, not matter what you can throw its way. Those $5,000 Wilsons, I've seen them consistently fail like their more reasonably priced base model 1911 cousins, because of dust, sand, moisture, you know the real-world, where you'll be fighting. Glock is the AK of Combat Handguns, they're nearly indestructible, their inexpensive and they always work.

It's like the iPhone. If given a choice and the cost was the same, would you choose the iPhone 1 or the iPhone 6? How about if I told you the iPhone 6 was actually less expensive, because that's the case for Glock. Since the Glock has less parts and its parts are made up from less expansive martial, they cost less. Since its creation nearly every major handgun manufacture has come up with their own versions to stay competitive. Some are decent alternatives; however, others are a complete waste of money.

The key when deciding on an alternate option, is to make sure it's as straightforward and isn't plagued by dangerous de-cocking buttons and catches and if at all possible doesn't have useless safeties.

If my life depended on it and all I had was a handgun, it would be a Glock 17. I'm not the only one. Since the 9-11 Attacks, our military has been exposed to up-close gunfights like never before, requiring the use have handguns. No more so than our courageous Special Operations units. Since that time, they too have begun to make the shift to the superiority and simplicity of the most practical handgun around. Check out the handgun being worn on the vest of the SEAL Team 6 Operator. Yes, that's right it's a Glock. These tactical professionals know, what matters most is NOT about taking the sexiest, coolest looking gun into battle, it's about the ability of accurately placing multiple rounds into their Threat in the shortest span of time, regardless of the circumstances, all the time, every time.

Multiplicity trumps size...

The second biggest controversy amongst avid firearms owners pertains to caliber choice. The argument can easily be condensed to the concept of 'Stopping Power'; a bullet or round's ability to 'Stop' a person dead in their tracks. So does caliber size actually make a difference? To a certain extent, caliber size does have a measured

effect downrange. Obviously a 20mm HE round can do tons more damage than a tiny BB pellet and 45 caliber projectile makes a bigger hole down range. However, simply because a particular round is bigger, doesn't mean it's better. When it relates to handgun battles, bigger is often worse. Tactically, the main objective of the handgun during a up close and personal fight, is to achieve as many hits on Threat in the shortest of time spans. It boils down to controllability due to the effects of recoil. In a fight, the more controllable a particular handgun is, the the less time it takes to accurately send another round. Yet, there is a point at which a particular caliber is simply too small to achieve the needed terminal damage down range. So the objective is to find that round which offers the most controllability, while still achieving adequate damage on your Threat.

The confusion has to do with a lack of understanding of the relationship between the dynamics of gunfights and its effect on ballistics as a whole. Too often people focus too heavily on 'Terminal Ballistics' which is only one component to the overall equation. Terminal Ballistics is the study of a given round's effect on the body itself to determine how fatal a particular round may be on impact. Obviously it's important to know the potential damage a particular round is capable of down range. The problem arises when people use Ballistics Gelatin tests, as means of determining fact and foretelling future.

Ballistics Gel is gel-like substance, which usually consist of a large rectangular cube, having the consistency of human flesh. The gelatin cube is typically about 10" x 10" x 20" and essentially becomes translucent bullet trap. It basically allows a person to see a bullet's performance through human like tissue. This would include its expansion upon impact, separation, wound cavity, trajectory and overall depth of penetration through simulated flesh. While ballistics gelatin is a great tool, it is also horribly deceiving. It leads people to assume conclusions, which simply can't be made with such limited scope of measurement.

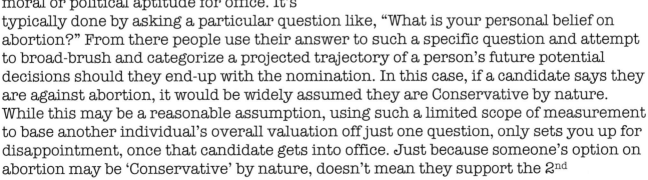

I liken Ballistic Gelatin tests to political Litmus tests. The Litmus test is method people use to determine a particular candidate's moral or political aptitude for office. It's typically done by asking a particular question like, "What is your personal belief on abortion?" From there people use their answer to such a specific question and attempt to broad-brush and categorize a projected trajectory of a person's future potential decisions should they end-up with the nomination. In this case, if a candidate says they are against abortion, it would be widely assumed they are Conservative by nature. While this may be a reasonable assumption, using such a limited scope of measurement to base another individual's overall valuation off just one question, only sets you up for disappointment, once that candidate gets into office. Just because someone's option on abortion may be 'Conservative' by nature, doesn't mean they support the 2nd

Amendment or even small government. In fact, there are many who would consider themselves 'Liberal' leaning, who do not support abortion as well. While a Litmus test may be useful in narrowing down a person's personal options, they are NOT some sort of fail proof crystal ball capable of predicting future outcomes.

What Ballistic Gelatin can NOT do, is evaluate terminal performance so as to articulate an overall valuation of effect, on the actual dynamics of a given fight itself. What this means is, a cube of 'Simulated' flesh, can't tell you how, chemicals and hormones like adrenalin, dopamine and say testosterone, effect a particular round's overall stopping capability. Nor can Ballistic Gelatin tests, speak to all the other factors associated with an actual fight against a violently attacking Threat. Just because a particular round appears to have devastating effects on simulated flesh, doesn't mean that round; in and of itself, has the ability to prevent a Threat from fighting 'Through' the pain, in spite of even a the most devastating wound.

A good example of this occurs all the time in forests across the world. Any experienced hunter could tell you that just because you shoot an animal in its heart and literally blow it apart with a rifle round, doesn't mean the animal will drop. In fact, deer and other animals can run for 5-minutes after such a devastating blow, especially if they're in the Rut and high on adrenalin and testosterone. Why, because there is a difference between the simple Cause of Death and the actual State of Being Dead. While a particular wound may be the actual Cause which brought death, in a gunfight, death most usually comes after the body has drained itself of blood. Similarly, a Red Stag in the Rut, could be shot though its heart and still be able to run a mile or more, before the 'Loss of Blood' shuts its body down, finally causing it to falls to its death.

What people so often assume, is that simply because the .45 ACP consistently shows a far bigger wound cavity than the 9mm Luger, that the .45 ACP must me a deadlier round. While I'll agree that (1) .45 ACP round may cause a more mortally fatal wound than the 9mm Luger, in an actual fight, the 9mm Luger is far more capable of being the more 'Deadly' option if applied correctly.

In the real-world, in real gunfights, especially when handguns are used, what stops a Threat is not how big the hole is but rather a particular round's Blood Loss Potential. Once the body's blood volume diminishes bellow a particular level, the body then becomes inoperable. It's when a body reaches this state of being, where the superhuman effects of adrenaline meet their match. When considering wound valuation at its most simplistic form, it's obvious that a bigger hole makes for a bloodier wound, so the bigger wound must mean the bigger round has a higher Blood Loss Potential. However, it's not that simple. To determine Blood Loss Potential, you must take into account a given round's Follow-up Rate. The concept of a given firearm's Follow-up Rate, has to do with how quickly the shooter is able to get back on Threat after recoil, for an 'Accurate' follow-up shot. So the mathematical expression for determining Blood Loss Potential, looks more like a trigonometry function as opposed to basic addition and subtraction.

Let's just say a .45 ACP has a wound cavity of 2-inches in diameter, where as a 9mm Luger only has a 1.5-inch diameter wound cavity. If the simple severity of the wound is

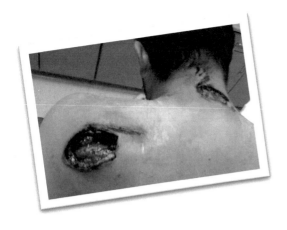

what's used to determine how deadly that wound is, and if the valuation is based off a number, then it's a simple comparison of the difference between wound cavities. So subtracting the difference would tell you the .45 ACP is the winner by half an inch.

However, when considering the effect that the dynamics of the fight has on the Threat's ability to fight through devastating wounds, you soon realize the math becomes a bit more involved. When a Threat's blood is flooded with chemicals and hormones, its effect gives them an almost superhuman-like ability to overcome injury and prolong the fight. Because of this reality, multiplicity of shots becomes an important factor and so we have to infuse a calculation for Follow-up Rate. Since we're comparing the 45ACP to the 9mm Luger, let's use the Glock 21 (45 ACP) and the Glock 17 (9mm) as our controls.

Since the 9mm Luger's recoil is less abrupt than the 45 ACP, it takes a Glock 17 shooter less time to accurately send their next follow-up shot. Studies have shown this to be around 1.5 times that of the 45 ACP. So with these numbers a more realistic equation for how 'Deadly' these rounds are, would look like this:

Blood Loss Potential

Follow-up Rate^2 x Wound Cavity = Blood Loss Potential

or

$FR^2 * WC = BLP$

Glock 21 (45ACP)
Follow-up Rate: 4 Rounds-Per Second
Wound Cavity: 2-inches
Score: 32 BLP

Glock 17 (9mm Luger)
Follow-up Rate: 6 Rounds-Per-Second
Wound Cavity: 1.5-inches
Score: 54 BLP

You'll notice something quite different about this equation, in that you're going to 'Square' the Follow-up Rate. The reason for this is to valuate the Shock Effect each additional round has to the Threat's Central Nervous System. It's this important factor that's so often overlooked.

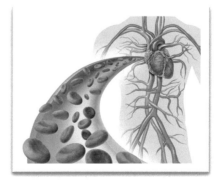

You see adrenaline and dopamine have and overriding effect on the Central Nervous System's electrical currents which run to your brain. When injury occurs, the nerves in that area scream out for help. That scream is echoed along an electrical current from the injury location to the brain and back. The body is designed to protect itself and maintain body function. So when your brain translates the scream into injury, it sends that message to the remainder of the body. What happens is the brain forces the body into a lower state much overall function. It then isolates the affected area, then goes about protecting that area from further damage, by intensifying the pain respecters of the nerves in that particular region. So when you break your leg, the brain tells the rest of the body to compensate, while also telling the affected leg to send excruciatingly sharp pain through the leg, if you attempt to bear weight on it. It's the 'Pain' which cause you to stop walking, thereby preventing further injury to that leg.

However, when adrenaline and other toxic chemicals and hormones are introduced, they override the body's pain mechanism. Giving you an ability to walk on a broken leg without feeling the as much pain. The more adrenalinly charged your Threat's blood is, the less pain he will feel. The less pain he feels, the less effect a particular injury has in its immediacy. To counteract the effects of adrenalin, you must increase the rate of damage on the system, or in other words, your rate-of-fire.

Here's why. There are countless stories of people being mortally wounded, yet still being capable of fighting in spite of their injuries. In fact, there are even cases where the Threat actually wins the fight 'After' being fatally shot. How's that? In these cases, the Threat receives a fatal wound, but continues to fight and kills the person who gave them that wound and then the Threat finally succumbs to his wound and also dies. It happens all the time for the very same reason a deer who's been shot, is capable of running a mile before they eventually fall and die.

For instance, I investigated a case where a suicidal lady killed herself approximately 2 ½ minutes after a Deputy literally blew her heart apart with a 1oz shotgun slug. She was able to keep shooting at the Deputies, sustaining (3) more gunshot wounds, until her body shutdown finally shutdown. At that point she collapsed to her back, shot herself (3) times in the chest and (2) times in the face, with the last shot to the face being ruled as the actual Cause of Death. What's interesting about this case, is that had she been wheeled into surgery immediately following the fatal shot to her heart, she would have still died.

The moral of the story comes down to the required need for immediately, massive blood loss. She stopped fighting only once her body had drained its self of the required supply of blood she needed to continue the fight.

If a gunfight, the objective is not Wound Size but rather Wound Effect. Your mission is to overload the Central Nervous System to such a degree, that it causes the other body's systems to go into Meltdown Mode and you must achieve this as quickly as possible. Meltdown Mode is most quickly achieved, through the multiplicity of wound infliction, within an extremely small time frame. In other words, the quicker you fill your Threat with 'Multiple' holes, the sooner he'll fall. It's the multiplicity of the infliction, which has the greatest overall effect.

Increasing your rate-of-fire, by sending multiple rounds into your Threats body in a short time span; one right after the other, gives each consecutive round an even greater Wound Potential than the one before it, thereby maximizing overall Wound Effect. The greater the 'Effect' a particular wound has on the body; the more overall Shock Effect it has on the Central Nervous System. The Shock Effect from the hydrostatic pressure associated with the wound cavity, decreases blood clotting thereby significantly thinning the blood itself. At the same time, it increases blood pressure, while also sending the heart rate through the roof.

The combined effect, when you introduce the multiplicity of gunshot wounds, very quickly becomes catastrophic. It's this combined Wound Effect, who's value is squared with each consecutive round, which causes blood to poor from effected areas, thereby maximizing total blood loss. So when comparing the 45 ACP to a much smaller 9mm Luger, with the more realistic Blood Loss Potential rating just listed, the 9mm Luger is capable of a much greater degree of Wound Effect, making the 9mm Luger a much more 'Deadly' round.

What this all means is that in a gunfight, the application of fire is what counts the most. The quicker you're able to continue the application of accurate fire, the sooner the battle is won. It's the veracity of your shots which places your Threat's body into a state of meltdown. Weather they die or not, well that depends on where you make those holes.

Round Selection...

What Gelatin does is simulate a given round's trajectory through human flesh. It gives you a wound value to work with. Even if that wound is catastrophic, such as the 1oz shot to the heart mentioned earlier, the fight WILL go on unless you fire-for-effect. The goal is to find a round that provides efficient retained weight as it passes through flesh, while at the same time offering less recoil so as to allow for a higher rate-of-fire.

The top three most popular handgun rounds are the .45 ACP, 40 S&W and 9mm Luger. All three are equally fatal. Why do I say this? Well a shot to the heart with either one will usually result in death. You can't exactly be deader than dead, so if they're all capable of causing death, then they must be equally fatal. However, as mentioned previously, the 9mm Luger is a better fighting round, since it has a higher potential for blood loos. That's why the Special Operations Community has adopted the 9mm Luger over both the .45 ACP and 40 S&W. The answer why is because the 9mm Luger is more practically effective for tactical purposes. The 9mm Luger is:

- Cost effective
- Easy to acquire
- Easiest to shoot
- Far more accurate

- Can be shot at greater distances
- Proper balance of overall Ballistics
- Offers the shooter more overall rounds per magazine

The goal in a gunfight is to WIN. Winning requires you to fight smarter not harder. The biggest problem with the .45 ACP and 40 S&W pertains to the 'Extra' effort a shooter must employ in order accurately place multiple rounds on their intended Threat.

The .45 ACP has an extremely slow and long recoil. What this means is it takes a considerable amount of time for the handgun's axis to resettle, meaning any rounds fired before it levels, are much more likely to completely miss the Threat. This also means it's a harder round to shoot in quick succession. The .45 ACP is also a very slow moving round. In fact, most people can actually see the round flying through the air when shooting at distances of 25 meters or greater. Due to its slow muzzle velocity, it is completely impractical at ranges over 50 meters. Why would you want to shoot further than 50 meters? Parking lots at the mall or corridors and hallways of office buildings are far greater than 50 meters. During an Active Shooter / Active Threat situation, you may need to engage a Threat at extended ranges. The .45 ACP is a bigger round meaning it costs more to produce. The other sacrifice to size is that they take up more room in your magazine, meaning you're left with far less rounds-per-mag than the 9mm Luger.

The 40 S&W's is a very interesting round altogether. In all honesty it's a science project gone bad. You would think since is smaller than the .45 ACP, then it must have less recoil. Unfortunately, that's not the case. While the .45 ACP's recoil rates higher in foot-pounds of energy, the 40 S&W's recoil is far snappier. Basically the 40 S&W is a .45 ACP in a 9mm package, meaning its recoil and ballistics as a whole, are completely unbalanced. This mean's the .45 ACP actually has more manageable recoil. On top of this, the 40 S&W's snappiness, makes it far less accurate in quick succession than the .45 ACP. The 40 S&W is also bigger than the 9mm, so it costs more and leaves the shooter with less rounds-per-mag. If you were to poll the average professional shooter, you'd find an overwhelming hatred of the 40 S&W altogether. You'll also hear those same people say the only reason they shoot the 40 S&W is because it's the one their agency or company chose.

Self-Defense Ammo...

Another misunderstood factor with ammunition selection has to do with the composition of the actual projectile itself. There are two predominant types of bullet compositions, the Full Metal Jacket (FMJ) or the Hollow Point (HP). Due to the Geneva Convention's rules on bullet type, the FMJ is by far the most commonly used worldwide. Like is usually the case, popularity does NOT mean the FMJ is better. What's interesting is why the United Nations made this distinction in the first place.

In the eyes of the U.N., an HP bullet is 'Inhuman'. Why, because it inflicts devastating bodily harm. Upon impact with flesh, an HP bullet rapidly expands like a star and rips its way through flesh, bone, organs and creates a massive wound cavity and exit wound. An FMJ on the other hand, retains a majority of its overall shape, passes through flesh, like a hot knife to butter and leaves a far less devastating exit wound.

The U.N. is in the business of Peace Keeping; they don't want armies killing each other. So they require armies to use inferior weaponry like the FMJ. However, the act of Combat itself is not about keeping peace it's about 'Making' peace. When it comes to Self-Defense, the person defending themselves is defending against an attack on their very existence. In this situation, death is not a possibility but rather a high and likely probability. So, the person defending themselves needs to kill their Threat quickly, so as to afford themselves the best chances of survival. So in a gunfight, killing your Threat before he's able to kill you, is your most paramount important objective.

Ironically hunters have historically opted for HP bullets because they have a higher potential of death, thereby making them not only more practical, but far more humane. The hunting world has perfected the act of killing animals, so that its done with ease and with speed. In all reality, a gunfight is no different than a hunt. Your Threat is hunting you and you are hunting your Threat. The only difference is that the animal you hunt walks upright and shoots back. You need to kill your prey as quickly as entirely possible and bullet choice directly effects the outcome. Choosing the right bullet will assist in achieving this goal with expeditious finality. However, choosing the wrong bullet in a gunfight, will prolong the fight itself, make it harder for you to win and exponentially increases your chances of death. When it comes to Self-Defense you require Personal Defense ammunition or HP bullets. Save the less expensive FMJ's for practice.

Top 3 Full-Size Combat Handguns...

The Full-Size Combat Handgun is hands down your best suited option. It affords the most ammunition, adequate grip, extended barrel length and is typically the most comfortable size to shoot while under rapidly fire. It's also the easiest to retain during a struggle. However, they are larger and heavy handguns and not typically the best Concealed Carry gun. Here are my Top 3 Glock style full-size options you should really consider.

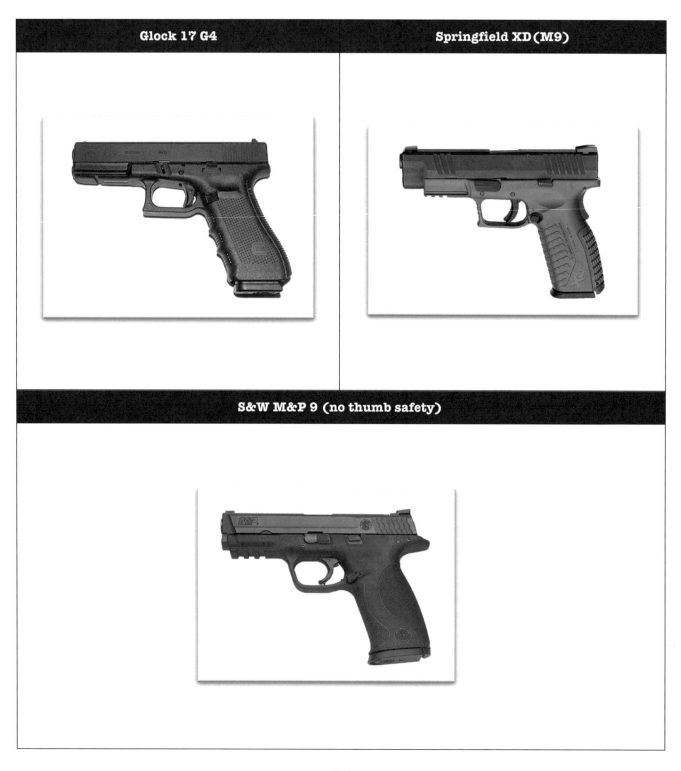

Top 3 Compact Combat Handguns...

The Compact Combat Handgun is your next best suited variant. It affords a decent balance of conceal ability, while still maintaining adequate ammunition, decent grip size and acceptable barrel length. While they are much easier to conceal than their Full-Size brothers, they are not as comfortable to shoot, especially for individuals with large hands. However, they fit a purpose and that is for the mission of conceal ability. Here are my Top 3 Glock style compact sized variants you should really consider.

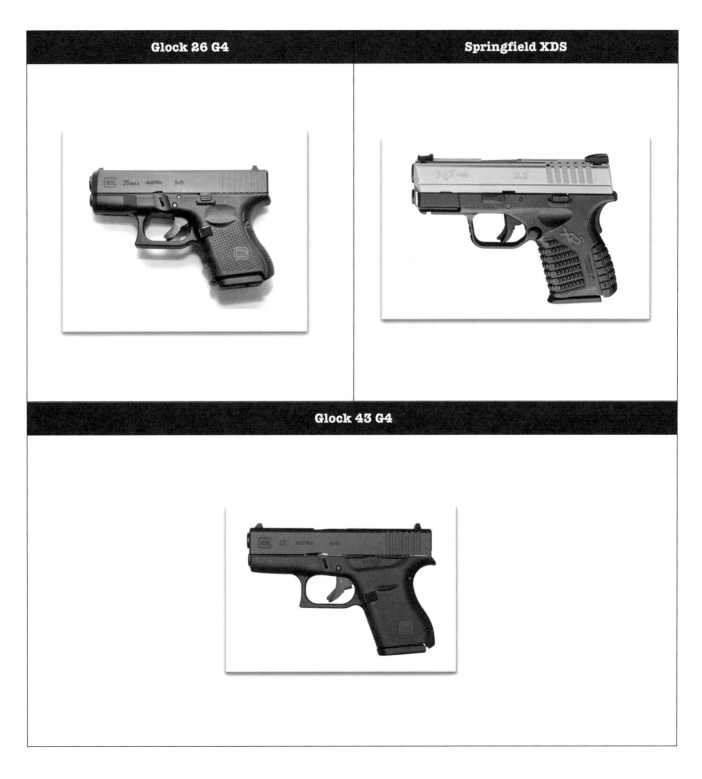

Top 3 Sub-Compact Combat Handguns...

The Sub-Compact Combat Handgun is your alternative for deep conceal ability. It affords the ability to easily carry a fighting style handgun with lightweight or formal attire, or even in a pocket. However, with such a scaled-down size, you will make some scarifies. These are by far the least comfortable to shoot, do not offer as many rounds and can be very finicky on ammunition. Yet they do serve their purpose and are your best alternative, when you require the greatest conceal ability. Here are my Top 3 Glock style sub-compact sized alternatives you should really consider.

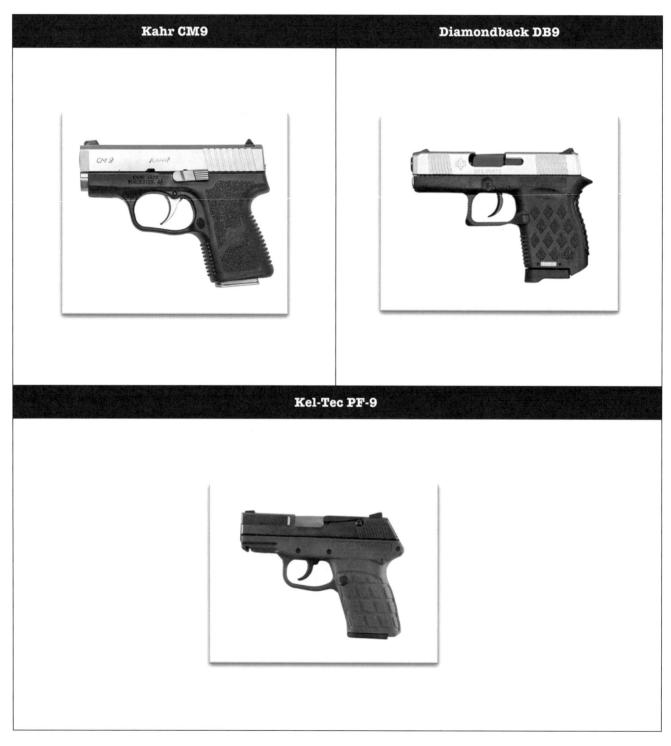

Top 3 Personal Defense Rounds...

There are dozens of ammunition manufactures around with hundreds of ammunition choices. It's important to understand that not all Personal Defense ammunition are created equal. When you go to war to save your life, you need to show up to that fight with the best ammunition capable of assisting in winning that fight. Cutting corners to for the least expensive box, is not a viable option. Doing so will increase the potential for firearms malfunctions during the fight, be less effective of actually killing your Threat and in turn, make the task of wining and surviving, a very difficult one. For this reason, I've selected three of the best Personal Defense rounds on the market and encourage you to fix your sights on one of these options. Keep in mind, Personal defense ammunition is expensive at about $1-2 a piece. You'll need to purchase enough to fill your main magazine and any spares you may carry. It's also important that you shoot at least (40) rounds before you start carrying a particular type of Personal Defense ammunition. This way you know that particular ammunition functions properly.

Top 3 FMJ Training Rounds...

When it's time to hit the range for training, you'll likely shoot dozens of rounds. If you're attending a training class, you may even shoot hundreds of rounds. Using Personal Defense ammunition for training could break your bank, since some Personal Defense rounds cost about $1-2 a piece. For this reason, you'll need to switch to a decent FMJ. There are dozens of ammunition manufactures who produce FMJ ammunition. The key is not to buy the cheapest option. The vast majority of lesser expensive ammunition, is made overseas and are NOT generally as safe. It's best to stick with proven manufactures who have a long safety record. It's also important to know that some handguns are very finicky, when it comes to FMJ ammunition. Since FMJ rounds are not produced to the same tolerances as Personal Defense ammunition, they have a tendency to cause malfunctions. So before you purchase in bulk, try a few boxes to assure they work well in your handgun. Here are three proven FMJ training options that operate superbly in most handguns.

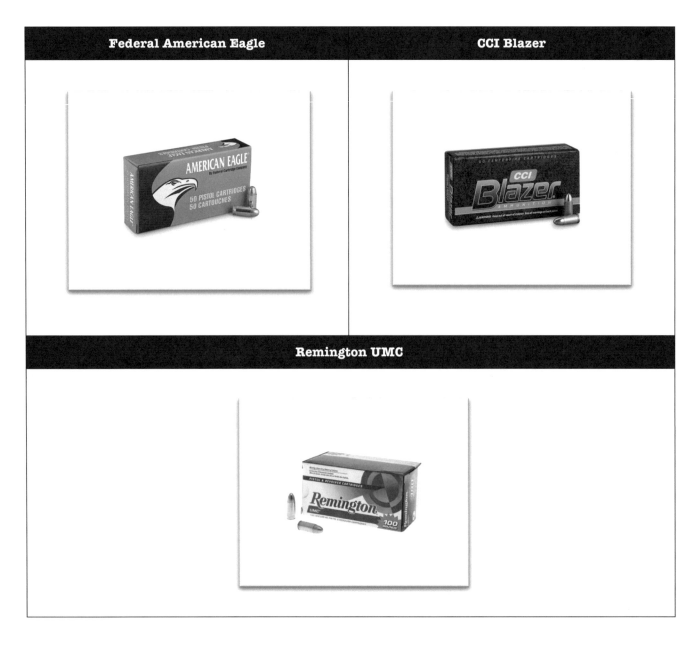

Top 3 Holsters...

Time is a commodity you do NOT have in a tactical environment. If you can't access your weapon and obtain a firm grip, you won't be able to fight with it. There are thousands of holster companies and tens of thousands of holsters out there. I have picked the following (3) for good reason.

When it comes to Concealed Carry, on the waist carry, is your most suitable option, with Inside the Waistband (IWB) being the most concealable. I have found the Alien Cloak Tuck 3.0 to be the most practical (IWB) holster in existence. There is a lot to be said about its versatility and adaptability, as well as being extremely affordable. It can also be adapted to an (OWB) rig.

Generally speaking, Outside the Waistband (OWB), carry is best suited for the range, duty and or tactical situations, as it does not provide ideal conceal ability. You should really consider the Blackhawk SERPA for (OWB) carry. The SERPA system is hands down the best tactical holster system in existence. It allows for multiple holster security level options, as well as a tactical light option. What takes the SERPA to a world of its own, is its ability to be used on multiple platforms from waist, vest, to drop-leg carry, via the SERPA Quick Disconnect Kit.

6

Handgun Safety

It goes without saying that firearms are an extremely vital, lifesaving tool during a deadly confrontation. Yet, they are inherently dangerous and should be handled with utmost care and safety, at all times. Most firearms injuries occur because of operator error and negligence, not by acts of violence. Generally speaking, a properly maintained firearm will not fire, unless the trigger is depressed on a loaded chamber. In fact, you could leave your firearm loaded and unattended for a hundred years and still it would not fire, unless someone or something manipulated its trigger. Recently, park rangers located a 130-year-old loaded Winchester rifle resting against a tree, in the middle of the Nevada wilderness. It had weathered the time of history and still it did not fire.

Just because you can leave a loaded firearm unattended and have confidence it will not self-combust, doesn't mean you should. This chapter is focused on Firearms Safety and how you can be the best most responsible firearms owner possible. Safety boils down to how the user uses and keeps their firearms. If you treat ALL firearms with respect at ALL times, keep them properly maintained and follow the ZuluSafe Cardinal Safety Rules, the likelihood of mishaps becomes almost nonexistent.

ZuluSafe Cardinal Safety Rules:

Firearms Safety is founded on the following (4) Cardinal Rules. Mechanical misfires are EXTREMELY rare with modern firearms. Religiously adhering to these rules will assure, that even under the unlikely circumstance of a misfire, your firearm will be pointed in a safe direction, thereby decreasing the chance of endangering your life or someone else's.

1. Treat ALL firearms as if they are ALWAYS loaded.

2. Keep your fingers OFF the trigger and OUTSIDE the trigger-guard until you are justified and ready to shoot.

3. NEVER point your muzzle at anything or anyone you're not justified and willing to kill.

4. Be SURE of your Threat and what stands beyond.

Maintenance & Cleaning:

The reason you own your handgun is to use it in aid of the defense of your life or someone else's. Firearms are 'Tools' and like tools, they do require general maintenance to assure they operate and fire without fail at ALL times. Their longevity is entirely up to how well you maintain them. You should inspect them frequently and clean them regularly.

- Always assure you read and follow the guidelines detailed in your firearm manufacture's user manual to a T. This is especially true when it comes to ammunition requirements and special circumstances.

- Be sure to inspect and clean your firearm after every firing, if exposed to moisture, dirt or once a month, whichever comes first.

- Take special care when inspecting or cleaning. This is when the vast majority of Negligent Discharges actually occur.

- Assure that your cleaning area is located in a secluded location, where you will not be distracted or interrupted.

- Make sure that any and <u>ALL</u> ammunition, is <u>COMPLETELY</u> removed from the cleaning area, <u>BEFORE</u> you begin cleaning.

- Pay special attention whenever you load and unload your firearm. Remember to be SURE of your Backstop. There have been many cases where individuals loading and unloading their firearms, have inadvertently shot their neighbors because they FORGOT about their backstop. For instance, people living in upstairs dwellings like apartments, forget that by pointing their weapon down, they're actually pointing it at their neighbors.

- Avoid detailed disassembly or full-stripping of your firearms. Leave this for your armorer. Doing so regularly, greatly decrease the lifespan of your firearm, especially if done incorrectly.

- Avoid custom modifications if at all possible. A quality Combat Handgun shouldn't require modifications. Doing so typically works against you in a gunfight and can actually compromise the safe operation of your firearm altogether.

- Annual inspection of ALL your firearms is important. Be sure to have this done by a qualified armorer in your area.

Security:

Maintaining proper security of your firearms is just as important as the the adherence to safety. Should something catastrophic occur with an 'Unsecure' firearm, Courts consistently view such an occurrence as Criminal Negligence. Being found

Criminally Negligent carries with it life altering, extremely protracted and extraordinarily expensive consequences. The responsibility of assuring that your firearms are secure, rests solely on your shoulders. Proper firearms security is a paramount priority, second only to firearms safety.

Types of Security

1. Direct Security is the most prudent form of firearms security. If your firearm is not on your person and in your 'Direct' control, it is not completely secure.

2. Mechanical Security is your most reasonable alternative to Direct Security. Any firearm not in your 'Direct' control, should remain under lock and key.

The concept of locking one's firearms may conflict with the vast majority of Armed America. It is however the most responsible manner of security and an extremely important concept to grasp. Every week, more and more people are injured and killed due to unsecure firearms. Sure firearms ownership has skyrocketed, but the cause for these incidents is not because of an increase on firearms ownership, but rather an increase in irresponsible ownership. Our Second Amendment gives us the right to own and carry firearms. However, it does not give us the right to be negligently irresponsible.

With that being said, there's long been a culture in America of stashing one's firearms in hiding places around the home, in hopes of defending against attack. The concept may appear to make sense on paper, however it's highly unlikely you'll actually be able to retrieve a firearm if it is not actually on your person. If say your seated on the couch and your front door is kicked in, you most likely won't have time to run and retrieve a firearm. Carrying your firearm on your person in your home may appear to be paranoid, but its actually the safest and quickest way to defend against attack. If, however you insist on stashing weapons around the home, you should consider purchasing a few GunValuts. They're compact, easy to use and fairly inexpensive. They also provide an adequate alternative that's practical during an attack.

Mechanical Security Options

1. The best type of locked Mechanical Security is a *gun safe*. There are a number of different types and sizes available. It really boils down to the size and quantity of your firearms. For instance, if you own long-guns, you'll need one of the free standing variants. If you simply own a handgun, you can get away with a much smaller less expensive option like a GunVault. Gun safes also come with multiple different types of locking mechanisms. I highly suggest a PIN code or finger impression variant. They are much more practical. If you value your firearms, it is highly suggested that you invest in a firesafe variant. While they are more expensive, they not only protect

against fire, but they're actually much more difficult to defeat should someone attempt to steal them.

2. Some people actually dedicate an entire room or walk-in closet as a glorified gun safe. This is handy and affords the owner plenty of room and storage space for all their firearms gear. Keep in mind though; this room must remain locked and secure at all times. Interior doors are also extremely easy to overcome. If you choose to dedicate a room like this as a gun safe, it is highly suggested that you upgrade the door to a much more secure thick exterior deadbolt type.

3. The next form of locked security is a locked gunbox. While this is much better than simply leaving the firearm out and fully accessible to kids, it does NOT prevent theft during a burglary. It is also very easy for a well determined child to break into, thereby defeating the purpose altogether.

4. The last example is a trigger / muzzle lock. Now days these are very common and are typically included with your purchase of a new firearm. While these are convenient and very inexpensive, they are extremely easy to defeat. These should be left for when you're transporting your firearms and only as a last resort.

Bullet Nomenclature:

The correct vernacular is actually 'Round'. As you can see from the image bellow, a 'Bullet' is a projectile and makes up but one small part of an actual Round, which you load into your firearm.

Round Function

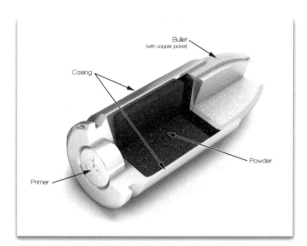

1. The Firing Pin strikes the Primer.

2. The Primer consists of a small cup filled with explosive. When struck, the Primer initiates the First Stage Explosion.

3. The Casing; which houses the Primer, directs the First Stage Explosion, upwards and towards the Powder Charge contained inside the Casing.

4. The First Stage Explosion ignites the Powder Charge, which initiates a Second Stage Explosion.
5. The energy of the Second Stage Explosion is directed to the base of the Bullet.
6. The Bullet is then forced out, fillies free from the Casing and down the Barrel.

Revolver Nomenclature:

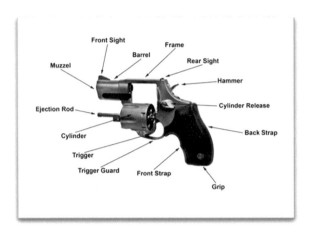

7. FRAME
    - Grip & Back Strap
    - Trigger
    - Trigger Guard
    - Hammer
    - Firing Pin
    - Cylinder Latch
    - Other Action Parts

8. BARREL
    - Rifled Bore (lands & grooves)
    - Front sight
    - Muzzle

9. CYLINDER
    - Extractor
    - Extractor Rod
    - Yoke / Crane

Revolver action types:

1. SINGLE-ACTION

    - The hammer is cocked, then light pressure on the trigger releases the hammer, which then flies free to strike the back of the firing pin.

2. DOUBLE-ACTION

    - Starts with a long, heavy trigger pull, which aligns the chamber and cycles / releases hammer.
    - This is by far the safer of the two actions. It greatly decreases chances of a Negligent Discharge in times of high stress.

How to safely inspect a Revolver:

1. Safely unload and remove all ammunition to a completely different area prior to inspection.
2. Repairing or other corrective actions MUST be performed per the manufacture's requirements, by a qualified armorer or gunsmith.
3. Check exterior for overall condition. (visible damage, rust or dirt)
4. Check stocks for damage or looseness.
5. Check exterior of barrel and bore for bulges, muzzle damage or obstructions.
6. Check to assure overall screws are tight and NOT backed-out or loose.
7. Check front and rear sights to assure they are NOT loose or damaged.
8. Check hammer nose / firing pin to assure against damage.
9. Check recoil plate and firing pin hole to assure against damage and or fouling.
10. Check extractor rod to assure it has smooth movement in and out.
11. Check extractor rod to assure it is tight. (can unscrew on S&W types)
12. Check the cylinder and chambers:

    - Front of cylinder is free of leading and fouling
    - Undersurface of extractor star is free of fouling, debris and oil
    - Chambers are clean and unobstructed
    - Cylinder opens and closes smoothly
    - Cylinder cycles smoothly and aligns / locks all chambers when dry firing (remember: safe direction & backstop when dry firing)

Semi-Auto Nomenclature:

Glock Style

Glock Fully Stripped

1911 Style

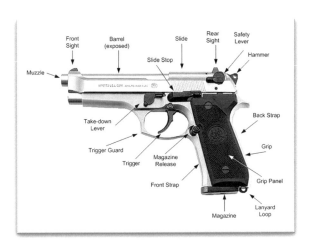

1911 Fully Stripped

Semi-Auto Components:

1. FRAME

    - Grip
    - Trigger
    - Trigger Guard
    - Magazine Well
    - Magazine Release
    - Ejector
    - Slide Stop

2. SLIDE

    - Front & Rear Sights

- Recoil Spring
- Recoil Guide
- Extractor
- Firing Pin
- De-Cocker (some models i.e. Beretta)

3. BARREL
   - Chamber
   - Bore (may be rifled or smooth depending on model)
   - Locking Lugs

4. MAGAZINE
   - Housing
   - Spring
   - Follower
   - But plate

Semi-Auto Action Types:

Semi-Autos differ from each other in how they function and or operate. Again, the more complicated the mechanism, the more inherent it is to both malfunction and safety hazards. Falling back on your understanding of Action vs. Reaction, the longer it takes you to disengage safeties and catches, the longer it takes you to fight. The longer it takes you to fight, the more rounds you're likely to absorb. The more rounds you absorb, the more likely you are to die. Its really that simple.

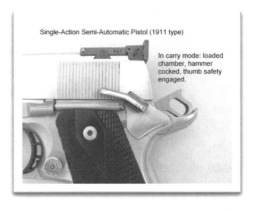

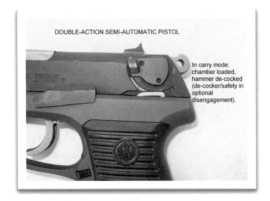

So, the more safeties and catches a given firearm has, the more complicated its Action and the less safe you actually are. Your 'Safety' is your brain and your habitual adherence to the ZuluSafe Cardinal Safety Rules. As mentioned before, I've been in many engagements where extremely experienced Operators have failed to fire their weapons, simply because they forgot to disengage safeties and catches. Manipulation of these mechanisms, require fine motor skills. As we've discussed previously, fine motor skills go out the window during real-world fights.

KISS and stick with a Glock style handgun for defensive purposes. I've literally shot nearly a million rounds through one of my Glocks and haven't had to replace a thing not

In carry mode: chamber loaded; trigger safety engaged

Striker Fired Semi-Automatic Pistol Glock Safe Action Type

even the recoil spring. I haven't even experienced a single mechanical malfunction. The only malfunctions I have experienced, have been due to ammunition or yaw. They may not look as sexy as a 1911, but they hold more ammo and could outlive ten 1911s. When you go to war, take a Glock, it won't let you down.

Manual De-cocking:

Manual De-Cocking is required on some Double-Action semi-autos and revolvers. The reason for this is to return the firearm to a safer state of being. When the hammer is fully cocked back on a Double-Action, the firearm reaches a state in which the firearm becomes a 'Hair-Trigger' firearm. What this means is the amount of reward pressure required to break the trigger sear, is minimal and often only takes a touch. However, returning the firearm to its 'Safe Mode' requires an EXTREMELY DANGEROUS manipulation of the hammer and trigger. In fact, performing this task violates the 2nd ZuluSafe Cardinal Safety Rule, which is to keep your finger OFF the trigger and outside the trigger-guard, until you are justified and ready to shoot. However, as you'll see, manual de-cocking without a de-cocker button, requires you to manipulate the trigger on a loaded chamber.

Proper De-Cocking

For firearms with built in de-cocking buttons:

1. Point the firearm in a safe direction with finger off the trigger and outside the trigger-guard.
2. Using you strong hand thumb, manipulate the de-cocker button by flipping it up or down according to the requirements for your particular firearm as seen in the images to your right.

For firearms without a built in de-cocking buttons:

1. Point the firearm in a safe direction with finger off the trigger and outside the trigger guard.
2. Place your support-hand thumb in between the hammer and hammer striker plate as shown in the image to your right.

3. Place your trigger finger on the trigger and apply reward pressure but do NOT press it all the way to the rear. At the same time, gently roll your support-hand thumb to allow the hammer to close towards the hammer striker plate until it is fully closed. As seen in the image to to your right.

4. Take your finger off the trigger and your firearm is de-cocked.
5. <u>DO NOT</u> use your thumb and index finger to manipulate the hammer. Doing so greatly increases the chances of a Negligent Discharge because the hammer is likely to slip from your grip.

<u>Improper De-Cocking</u>

This is where the majority of Negligent Discharges occur. For this reason, it is highly suggested that you steer clear of any firearm which requires such a manipulation. Even those models which offer a built in button, require an internal manipulation of the hammer and trigger mechanisms and thus still pose a risk of a Negligent Discharge. Firearms which require de-cocking pose a SERIOUS risk to your safety, especially during times of high stress. I have personally witnessed dozens of Negligent Discharges during moderate stress courses of fire by well experienced Operators. Why? As we've previously discussed, the higher the stress, the less ability you have to perform fine motor functions. Add a bit of sweat, grim and fatigue and you have the perfect recipe for disaster. The Glock style weapon is so simple and safe you just can't go wrong. Stick with a Glock and avoid complicated firearms.

How to safely inspect a semi-auto:

1. Safely unload and remove all ammunition to a completely different area prior to inspection.

   - Point firearm in a safe direction and engage safeties if present

- Remove the magazine
- Clear the chamber
- Visually and physically inspect (look & feel) the chamber and magazine well to assure the firearm is completely empty (nothing to feed it, nothing to eat)
- Repeat this two more times

2. Repairing or other corrective actions MUST be performed per the manufacture's requirements by a qualified armorer or gunsmith.

3. Perform a Function Check.
    - Dry-fire and hold the trigger to the rear. Pull the slide rearward and allow it to almost close. Release the slide. It should return to battery on its own
    - Release the trigger. It should completely re-set on its own
    - Rack the slide. If you have a hammer, put it in the down position. Insert an UNLOADED magazine. Rack the slide. The slide should lock open
    - Press the magazine release button and hold it in. The magazine should fall free or release
    - Insure safeties cocker's and all other catches are functioning properly.

4. Check the barrel and bore for bulges, cracks, muzzle damage, rust, fouling and obstructions.

5. Check the stock to assure it is not too loose or damaged.

6. Check all magazines for dents, cracks, broken welds, deformed feed lips, loose base plates and other forms of damage.

7. Check the frame for ejector damage, cracks holes, notches other damage and damage to the magazine well.

7
Loading & ReLoading

Praise the Lord and pass the ammunition! If you survive a gun battle, you'll be doing a lot of praising the Lord. However, first you need to win that fight and ammunition is vital to that end. Feeding and keeping your firearm fed, is an essential component in winning a gunfight. As we've already discussed, most gunfights involve the expenditure of multiple rounds. If you're wise, you'll carry one or two extra loaded magazines. The idea is that you're expecting the worst case scenario, like an Active shooter / Active Threat situation or even a Terrorist Act. Regardless, you've planed a way to stay in the fight and a practical surplus of ammunition is the best way to do this. Your level of proficiency with loading and reloading, should be as simple as clapping your hands. The best way to master this, is through repetitive training and the ZuluFight Dry-Fire Training System, is the most effective way to accomplish this task. Be sure to secure your copy. Dedicate some time to mastering your reloads, so you're ready for that worst case scenario.

Loading:

Loading your semi-auto handgun is as easy as 1, 2, 3. Simply insert a loaded magazine into the magazine well located in the grip of your handgun. Then slap the bottom of the magazine to assure it's properly seated. Finally rack the slide to chamber a round and you're ready to go.

To Properly Load Do The Following:

NOTE: Stage index finger on business end of Snap-Cap. This allows for more consistent loading while also assuring Snap-Cap is in correct position.

NOTE: Firmly and generously tap the bottom of the magazine to assure it is properly seated.

NOTE: Get into the habit of sweeping ejection port while obtaining grip of your slide when attempting to rack. This allows your brain to encode one solid movement for both Type 2 Malfunction clearing and normal racking.

NOTE: ALWAYS obtain an over-handed firm grip towards rear of slide. Assure finger is outside trigger guard. Push forward with gun hand while pulling back with support hand to rack slide.

NOTE: Release grip of slide after pulling it all the way to the rear. Allow slide to slam forward on its own while also allowing support hand to naturally fling back towards chest. This assures your first round will properly load.

Combat Reload:

A Combat Reload is what's needed when your gun goes dry during a gunfight. Most semi-auto firearms will lock back and stay open, to indicate that its mouth is open and ready to be fed. To feed it simply depress the magazine release, strip the empty magazine, retrieve a new one and repeat the previous mentioned loading sequence to get back into the fight.

To Perform A Proper Combat Reload Do The Following:

NOTE: Start by slightly canting firearm to allow for visual inspection of ejection port to identify stoppage. Also bring arms back allowing elbows to naturally rest on upper abdomen. This creates a natural working platform to work from allowing you to focus on your Threat while placing firearm in direct focal plane to allow you to still see your firearm utilizing peripheral vision.

NOTE: Retrieve and Stage index finger on business end of Snap-Cap. This allows for more consistent loading while also assuring Snap-Cap is in correct position.

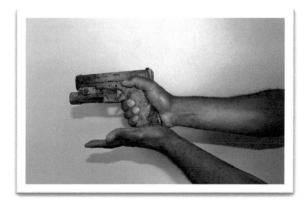

NOTE: Firmly and generously tap the bottom of the magazine to assure it is properly seated.

NOTE: Get into the habit of sweeping ejection port while obtaining grip of your slide when attempting to rack. This allows your brain to encode one solid movement for both Type 2 Malfunction clearing and normal racking.

NOTE: ALWAYS obtain an over-handed firm grip towards rear of slide. Assure finger is outside trigger guard. Push forward with gun hand while pulling back with support hand to rack slide.

NOTE: Release grip of slide after pulling it all the way to the rear. Allow slide to slam forward on its own while also allowing support hand to naturally fling back towards chest. This assures your first round will properly load.

Tactical Reload:

This is a reload performed during a tactical lull in the battle. The intent of a Tactical Reload is to top-up your firearm with more food, just in case the battle continues.

To Perform A Proper Tactical Reload Do The Following:

NOTE: Stage magazine so business end is faced away from body. Obtain grip at bottom of magazine placing it between index and middle finger while opening and extending thumb.

NOTE: Remove simulated partial magazine from firearm first by placing it in web of thumb. Then insert simulated fresh magazine.

NOTE: Firmly and generously tap the bottom of the magazine to assure it is properly seated.

8
Malfunction Mitigation

Malfunctions are an inevitable occurrence and something you NEED to prepare for. Since you're training for a fight, it's extremely important to understand its dynamics. One of those happens to be firearms malfunctions. They can occur for a number of reasons. During a fight though, the top (3) reasons have to do with either physical contact with your Threat or yaw effect due to extreme movement or failing to apply proper grip while firing. There are (3) basic types of malfunctions and (1) Catastrophic occurrence. The forth is a mechanical failure rendering your firearm useless. While this is rare, it does occur, which is why you would also need to know other means of Self-Defense such as Krav Maga.

Type 1 Malfunction:

A Type 1 Malfunction is the most basic. There are two kinds of Type 1 Malfunctions:

- A misfire
- Slide closes on empty chamber

A misfire typically occurs because of either a poor round or damaged firing-pin. The second Type 1 typically occurs during the course of shooting, when the shooter accidently engages the magazine release and the magazine falls out of battery thereby preventing the next round from entering the chamber.

To Fix A Type 1 Malfunction Do The Following:

NOTE: Start by slightly canting firearm to allow for visual inspection of ejection port to identify stoppage. Also bring arms back allowing elbows to naturally rest on upper abdomen. This creates a natural working platform to work from allowing you to focus on your Threat while placing firearm in direct focal plane to allow you to still see your firearm utilizing peripheral vision.

NOTE: Firmly and generously tap the bottom of the magazine to assure it is properly seated.

NOTE: Get into the habit of sweeping ejection port while obtaining grip of your slide when attempting to rack. This allows your brain to encode one solid movement for both Type 2 Malfunction clearing and normal racking.

NOTE: ALWAYS obtain an over-handed firm grip towards rear of slide. Assure finger is outside trigger guard. Push forward with gun hand while pulling back with support hand to rack slide.

NOTE: Release grip of slide after pulling it all the way to the rear. Allow slide to slam forward on its own while also allowing support hand to naturally fling back towards chest. This assures your first round will properly load.

Type 2 Malfunction:

A Type 2 Malfunction is easily identified by the spent casing which hangs from the ejection port. This is the most common malfunction in Combat situations due to a constantly changing shooting position. This typically occurs from yaw due to extreme movement or failing to apply proper grip while shooting.

To Fix A Type 2 Malfunction Do The Following:

NOTE: Start by slightly canting firearm to allow for visual inspection of ejection port to identify stoppage. Also bring arms back allowing elbows to naturally rest on upper abdomen. This creates a natural working platform to work from allowing you to focus on your Threat while placing firearm in direct focal plane to allow you to still see your firearm utilizing peripheral vision.

NOTE: Firmly and generously tap the bottom of the magazine to assure it is properly seated.

NOTE: Obtain grip of your slide and sweep the stuck case free as you rack.

NOTE: ALWAYS obtain an over-handed firm grip towards rear of slide. Assure finger is outside trigger guard. Push forward with gun hand while pulling back with support hand to rack slide.

NOTE: Release grip of slide after pulling it all the way to the rear. Allow slide to slam forward on its own while also allowing support hand to naturally fling back towards chest. This assures your first round will properly load.

Type 3 Malfunction:

A Type 3 Malfunction is much more difficult to overcome and requires extra time. Meaning you'll have to move to cover, while mitigating this stoppage. This kind of malfunction almost exclusively occurs due to a faulty magazine. Basically the magazine spring losses it's springiness and fails to apply the required pressure that pushes rounds into your firearm's chamber. This is a VERY bad malfunction during a gunfight as it will take you out of the fight for a while. If you notice this type of malfunction while training, repair, discard or replace the magazine prior to carrying it for defensive use.

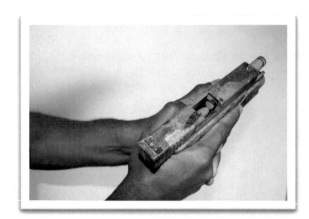 

To Fix A Type 3 Malfunction Do The Following:

NOTE: Start by slightly canting firearm to allow for visual inspection of ejection port to identify stoppage. Also bring arms back allowing elbows to naturally rest on upper abdomen. This creates a natural working platform to work from allowing you to focus on your Threat while placing firearm in direct focal plane to allow you to still see your firearm utilizing peripheral vision.

NOTE: Remove simulated partial magazine from firearm. This will be a difficult task since the first round is wedged in the chamber. You'll need to use diligent force.

NOTE: Now you'll need to violently rack your slide back and forth a few times to free the stuck round.

NOTE: Stage index finger on business end of Snap-Cap. This allows for more consistent loading while also assuring Snap-Cap is in correct position.

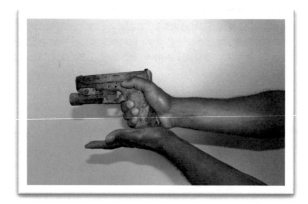

NOTE: Firmly and generously tap the bottom of the magazine to assure it is properly seated.

NOTE: Get into the habit of sweeping ejection port while obtaining grip of your slide when attempting to rack. This allows your brain to encode one solid movement for both Type 2 Malfunction clearing and normal racking.

NOTE: ALWAYS obtain an over-handed firm grip towards rear of slide. Assure finger is outside trigger guard. Push forward with gun hand while pulling back with support hand to rack slide.

NOTE: Release grip of slide after pulling it all the way to the rear. Allow slide to slam forward on its own while also allowing support hand to naturally fling back towards chest. This assures your first round will properly load.

Type 4 Malfunction:

A Type 4 Malfunction is the most difficult to overcome and should be considered a catastrophic mechanical failure of your firearm. This essentially renders your firearm completely inoperable, meaning you'll have to find another way to defend yourself. This kind of malfunction usually occurs due to a combination of faulty ammunition and or poor cleaning. The result is either a stuck casing in the breach or a lodged round in the barrel called a 'Squib Load'. Both outcomes require complete disassembly and tools to repair the stoppage. If you experience this type of malfunction during a gunfight, you have two choices. Either take the fight to the Threat physically or tactically re-deploy to cover.

9
Basic Marksmanship

Your journey to becoming an efficient tactical marksman begins by first mastering the skills of a basic marksman. Marksmanship pertains to how well your body is able to marry itself to your weapon. Obtaining proficiency in the higher tempo arena of tactical marksmanship, means you've first learned the art of making your weapon an extension of yourself. That journey starts with mastering the following important techniques. The ZuluFight Dry-Fire Training System is key to this journey and will make the task of mastery an easier one.

1. Stance
2. Grip
3. Sight Alignment
4. Sight Picture
5. Breathing
6. Trigger Control
7. Follow Through
8. Trigger Reset

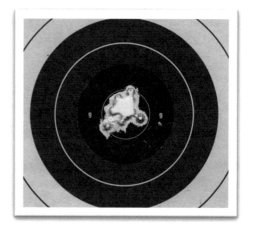

Stance:

Consistent and accurate shots down range begin with your base. Your base is what founds you to the ground it's what allows you to absorbed recoil. Without this base, your house comes troubling down. There are a number of different marksmanship stances available to you. The one that feels the most natural though is typically the best one for you.

Weaver Stance

The Weaver Stance is one of the more basic types of stance and the most common stance you'll find on shooting ranges. This stance is achieved by:

- Standing sideways from your target with your support shoulder facing your target.

- Your shooting arm crosses in front of your chest and is fully extended perpendicular to your support shoulder. This arm is used to absorb the forces of recoil and acts as the "Pushing" force of the stance.
- Your support arm is slightly bent with your elbow out to 9 O'clock. This arm provides the "Pulling" force of the stance.
- By Pushing with your strong arm and pulling back equally with your support, you create an extremely stable vise like grip.
- Easily acquired.
- Easily maintained for very extended periods of time
- The most accurate stance if only shooting "ONE" shot.
- Very difficult to accomplish tactical movement while also maintaining this type of stance.

Isosceles Stance

The Isosceles Stance derives its name from the shape of the shooter's arms. It is vastly different to the Weaver and most common amongst tactical shooters. This stance is achieved by:

- Squarely facing your target.
- Feet shoulder width apart.
- Slight bend at the knees with weight forward and over the balls of your feet.
- Arms locked straight forward forming the "Isosceles" triangle.
- Recoil is absorbed in both arms with the axis of recoil going in towards your chest.
- Easily acquired.
- Very easy to move while also maintaining a level shooting platform.
- Difficult to maintain for an extended period of time as it will cause your arms to eventually tier.

Natural Fighting Stance

This stance is the one which comes natural to you, and is the one you'll most certainly instinctively resort to upon attack. It's typically a slight modification of both the Weaver and the Isosceles and is similar to that of a basketball player's defensive stance. This type of stance is commonly referred to as the 'Modified Isosceles'. It should mirror the stance you resort to in a fight also known as your 'Tactical Stance'. Your dominant leg is typically the one that's slightly forward, with feet almost shoulder width apart. Your body is also in a slightly crouched or squatted position. This stance should offer you the following:

- STABILITY: Provides the proper balance left, right, backwards and forwards so as to absorb recoil, as well as punches, kicks or serious contact with your Threat during an up close and personal battle.

- MOBILITY: Provides the ability to naturally move left, right, backwards or forwards and at angles without trouble. Also provides ease of torso rotation at the waist, giving you the ability to track your Threat and shoot without moving your base.
- BALANCE: Balances both stability and mobility for an all-around fighting stance. To test this, acquire your stance then have someone push you from all angles to assure your base remains firm.

Tactical Fighting Stance

Natural Shooting Stance

Grip:

Your grip is a huge factor in your ability to absorb recoil and control the movement; or flip, of your firearm under recoil. This is especially true during multiple round engagements. When you depress the trigger and your firearm fires, it actually moves before the round exits the barrel. The more grip you apply as you fire will decrease the overall movement of your firearm in recoil, thereby allowing the bullet to fly straighter and flatter and much more accurately round to round.

The effects of recoil are very similar to that of water under hydraulic pressure. The pressure; or recoil, will follow the path of lest resistance. Proper grip is accomplished by first obtaining a solid grip with your strong or shooting hand. Next your support hand fills the gaps left on the opposite side of the firearm's handle or grip with both thumbs resting against each other.

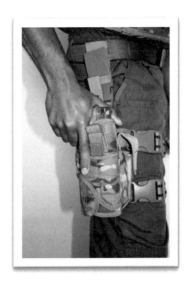

NOTE: Your first grip should be your last. Assure firearm is gripped high in web of thumb & trigger finger is staged outside trigger guard.

NOTE: The higher your grip is on your firearm, the closer it is to the axis of recoil. The closer your grip is to this point, the more egomaniacal your grip is, the easier it is to maintain and the better aligned your wrists, arms, shoulders and torso is to absorbing the recoil. This prevents the recoil from being directed over your arms which makes the firearm a lot snappier from round to round. 70% of grip should come from fingers of support hand. This allows for consistent & uninhibited trigger squeeze.

Sight Alignment:

Sight Alignment is achieved by equally aligning your front sight post with your rear sight notch. An easy way to remember this is 'Equal Height & Equal Light' Your front post is equal in height to your rear sight and there is equal light on each side of your front post. If your front sight post is positioned too far to the right, your bullet will strike right. If it's positioned too far up, your bullet will strike high.

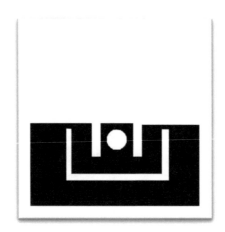

Sight Picture:

Sight picture is the relationship between your perfectly aligned sights and your target or Threat. It's the action of overlaying your aligned sights and putting them where you wish to hit your Threat. For purposes of Basic Marksmanship, your front sight should be your focal point and in perfect focus, while your Threat should appear slightly blurred. In this case your bullet will strike just above your front sight post.

Breathing:

Proper oxygenation of your bloodstream is very important. Maintaining proper oxygenation levels will allow your muscles to work as they are supposed to. Holding your breath will cause your hands to trimmer and your eyes to lose focus. You should breath as normal as possible and when possible, shoot at the natural pause between breaths.

Trigger Control:

It's been said that 80% of accuracy deficiencies downrange is due to poor trigger control. Your trigger finger should 'Squeeze' the trigger, not pull or jerk it back. You should maintain consistent rearward pressure and speed all the way through the trigger squeeze. Typically, the best accuracy is achieved by using only the pad of your trigger finger. So avoid the urge of wrapping your whole finger around the trigger.

Follow Through:

Follow through is the concept of squeezing the trigger all the way rearward past the point at which the firearm discharges. Follow through is more of a cognitive thought than an action. It's a reminder to continue the 'Squeeze' past recoil. As the firearm flips back, you release the squeeze to Trigger Reset, allowing the firearm to fall back into alignment with your Threat.

Trigger Reset:

This is accomplished by slowly moving your trigger finger forward after Follow Through. Approximately halfway forward you will hear your trigger click and may even feel it. This is where your trigger resets and the position at which it is ready to be squeezed rearward again. Getting used to the position of your trigger's reset will greatly increase your overall accuracy due to the fact that it requires less overall movement.

Driving your Trigger:

When shooting multiple rounds, it's important to understand and become familiar with the 'Rhythm of Recoil', the pattern by which your firearm acts as it flips back and returns to rest and how that relates to trigger manipulation. This can be best understood by likening it to driving a car at high speeds around a tight corner. Too much gas; or jerky trigger pulling, and you'll spin out. Hit the brakes and you'll fishtail. Too much movement of the steering wheel and you'll lose control.

Mastering your firearm's Rhythm of Recoil is like mastering your car's RPM's. You must learn to input an appropriate amount of speed on the trigger, with just the right amount of grip combined with enough forward pressure and leaning on the firearm to allow your firearm the ability to fall back into alignment with your Threat for a level shooting platform for your next shot. Jerking the trigger will only cause you to shoot wildly, making accuracy a hopeless task.

10
Situational Awareness
&
Threat ID

If you can't see your Threat, you can't beat your Threat. Threat Identification is an extremely important process and will greatly affect the outcome of your battle. Just as important as it is to identify your Threat, it's also important to know who's a Threat and who's not. When bullets start flying, the last thing you wanna do is turn around and blast granny by accident, when the guy who's shooting at you is actually standing next to her. This is why 'Situational Awareness' goes hand in hand with Threat Identification.

For the most part, your Threat is likely to be within arm's reach, however there are times when you could be attacked from across a room or even across a parking lot. There are also external factors such as low light, fog or even bright light, which could greatly diminish your ability to see your Threat. For these reasons it's vitally important that you develop the ability to correctly identify a Threat. It's also extremely important that you train your eyes to 'Seek'.

While this may sound straightforward, its actually not. If you lean back on your understanding from Chapter (2) of what happens physiologically during a fight, you'll realize just how difficult it is to differentiate things, while under attack, let alone to 'Seek' clarity and definition of the vastness of your environment. The best way to help train your eyes to 'Seek' is by incorporating ABC's Tactical Training Aides into your training sessions. To learn more about ABCs Tactical Awareness Aides, turn to Page 134.

DELTA Threat ID:

The most tactically effective Threat Identification technique was developed by the United States Special Forces. This five step process; when practiced, will assure you appropriately scan your environment the right way.

1. **Whole Body**: The first step is to cognitively thinking about 'Who' you're actually looking at. Is it a man or woman, adult or child? Who are they? Are they in a uniform? Do they have a badge? Could they actually be a friend? These are all very important questions one must train their minds to 'Think' while their eyes 'Seek'. Seeing a person's 'Whole Body' will help elevate the chances of you mistaking a friend for a foe.

2. **Hands:** Your next step is to find their 'Hands'. It's been said "It's the hands that kill." Finding someone's hands will aid in determining if the possible threat is armed or not. Are they armed with a weapon or holding a cell phone? Seeing a weapon does NOT mean to 'Shoot' or that they're a threat. They could actually be assisting you or a police officer. This is why all five steps are important.

3. **Waistband:** Now it's time to check their waistband. If you didn't see a weapon in their hand, it doesn't mean they're not hiding one on their waist or in their waistband. Visual check their waist. What are they wearing, could something be hidden there? These are questions you should be asking.

4. **Arm Span:** After this you need to check their immediate surroundings. Is there anything in there 'Reach' which could be used as a weapon? This will also give you the ability to identify other persons and or other potential hazards.

5. **Demeanor:** Lastly, you need to check their face and body language. This is the most overlooked step and usually be the key to uncovering the truth. Remember 90% of communication is 'Non-Verbal' meaning body language often times says all. You should be asking yourself if they appear happy, sad or even angry? Look into their eyes, are they letting off that they're hiding something or being tricky? Or does their demeanor tell you they're an innocent bystander or an armed citizen attempting to aid in your defense?

Each of these steps are extremely important in assuring that you correctly identify a Threat. Remember the most overlooked step is 'Demeanor'. You need to confirm that they actually 'Look' like a Threat, either through their facials or body language. Becoming proficient in this technique requires practice. It's most easily achieved during Stress Inoculation training like Force on Force Training simulations. However, an easy way start building solid Threat Identification habits, is by actively identifying random people on a daily basis. Follow the SOF Threat ID process as you interact with other people on a daily basis. Ask yourself if the random person approaching you is a 'Threat'? then follow the five easy steps. Doing this on a regular basis will cause your mind to develop a habit of always scanning your environment for possible threats and will keep you situationally aware at all times.

'Look' at what you're supposed to 'See':

The next area of importance is to 'Look' at what you're supposed to 'See'. What this means is, once you identify a Threat, focus on them. At that point nothing in the entire universe matters more that the person who's trying to kill you. It's vital that you can accurately read and track the Threat and determine their level of risk to your life. Looking at your gun-sights will <u>NOT</u> help you. Searching for your gun-sights will only distract you. Instead, track your Threat, identify their movements and begin the process of calculating their actions. This can only be achieved by maintaining optical clarity of your Threat. In a gunfight, Traditional Sight Alignment and Sight Picture are completely useless to you. Instead obtain a ZuluFight Sight Picture.

Traditional Sight Picture

NOTE: Traditional Sight Picture. Sights in focus while threat is out of focus.

NOTE: ZuluFight Sight Picture. Threat is in focus while sights are out of focus.

The easiest way to understand this is to find a picture on a wall. Focus on a particular part of the image. Now point at the exact spot your looking and maintain visual clarity of the image, not your finger. Now cognitively identify your outstretched arm. You should barely notice your pointed finger which is blurry yet pointing at the exact spot you were looking. Aiming your gun at your threat in a gunfight is no different. Tell me something, do you look at your finger when you ring a door bell or do you focus on the door bell? It's the same thing. Present your firearm and ring your threat's door bell. You know that large thing protruding from the center of your Threat's face, just above his upper lip? That's his bell, so ring it!

Situational Awareness:

Maintaining a high level of 'Tactical Awareness' will assure that you are not just effective in identifying possible threats, but that you're also 'Aware' of your surroundings. Being aware of what's around you, will aid in your ability to locate places of cover, potential hazards, bystanders, backdrops or even arriving police officers. What it will also do is allow you to find your Threat's homeboys, who may be attempting to flank you during an attack.

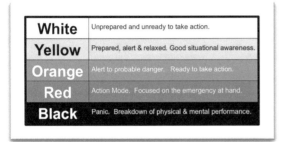

A tactical genius by the name of Col. Jeff Cooper, simplified a pretty practical approach to the concept of a Tactical Awareness by developing a color code of different mental awareness levels. He determined that to be ready for the randomness of an ambush, one must maintain a level of heightened neutrality. Meaning one must not be completely at rest. Otherwise that individual could be taken by 'Complete' surprise and upon attack, would easily revert to panic and would most certainly be doomed to defeat. He determined that by maintaining a balanced level of heightened neutrality, where one is prepared yet still relaxed, they could easily transition to a level of 'Alertness' and then 'Action' without reverting to complete panic and fear.

Being Situationally Aware, means your head is on a swivel and you're constantly scanning your environment. It means you're 'Seeking' to 'Identify' potential Threats both near and far. This is a skill that takes a ton of work for most people. For those of us fortunate to grow-up in the inner-city, we developed a high sense of awareness also called 'Street Smarts'. However, if you grew-up in the suburbs or out in the sticks, you'll likely struggle in this area. Don't lose hope, becoming proficient with this, can be done. It starts by actively scanning your environment at all times. That means when you walk out of a door, scan left then right just as you would when entering a roadway. When walking through the park, scan, look for potential Threats. Learn to use your peripheral vision and identify people who approach you. Train your peripheral awareness by determining if the person approaching or passing you is a Threat, without actually looking at them. Over time your overall level of Tactical Awareness will heighten and you'll develop the 'Habit' of being aware.

11
Multi-Threat Engagement

Should you find yourself reacting to a deadly Threat, it's extremely likely you'll be faced with not one, but multiple Threats. Criminals are like wolves, they lurk in wait for helpless sheep and like wolves, they tend to travel in packs. This is why it's vitally important that you develop the habit of 'Situational Awareness'.

During a recent Active Shooter incident at a Las Vegas Walmart, an armed citizen learned this lesson the hard way. While sneaking-up on who he thought to be the 'Only' Active Shooter, the brave citizen ended-up getting flanked and gunned down by a second Active Shooter. While his actions were heroic, his death was most unfortunate and just may have been prevented had he assumed that there are ALWAYS multiple Threats.

As a Sniper, I learned to blend in and be sneaky. Over a period of time, I acquired an acute ability to become a Chameleon of sorts and operate undetected and unhampered in a variety of environments. This ability was founded on ONE principle. To remain unseen, you must first assume that someone is ALWAYS watching and that someone is an enemy Sniper who's about to shoot you in your face. This mindset means that every movement a Sniper makes, is taken with utmost care and is calculative by nature. It's as though you can literally feel the enemy Sniper's Mil-Dot Reticle resting on your face, causing your nose to itch.

In a similar way, you must ALWAYS assume there are multiple Threats at different angles, distances and behind EVERY blind spot. This degree of Tactical Awareness is assured to keep you in a state of readiness as you actively 'Seek' for Threats....plural.

Effective use of senses:

Identifying multiple Threats comes down to how well you use your senses. You must assure that you are reminding yourself to both 'Look' and 'Hear' the Threats who stalk you. As discussed previously, our bodies will experience a number of physiological effects when confronted with a deadly Threat. Due to the effects of Tunnel or Focused Vision, you will have a tendency to see only the Threat that's directly in front of you.

Under extremely stressful situations like this, our ears are tethered to our eyes. Essentially they are hearing what our eyes are seeing.

The problem arises when you consider the likelihood of multiple Threats. If your eyes are laser focused on one individual, and due to the Laws of Combat, you've lost your peripheral vision, how in the world will you even see the other Threats?

The answer is by 'Resetting' your brain. Our brains are divided into multiple sections. For the most part though, we have a left and right side. Our sensory System is spider webbed throughout both sides of our brain. During times of extreme focus, it's important to 'Reset' allowing your brain the ability of regaining its Spatial Awareness. Similar to Situational Awareness, your Spatial Awareness allows you to understand the relation of thing to one another within your immediate vicinity. Your ability to regain a Spatial balance is essential if you're wanting to differentiate between one Threat and another.

This is best accomplished by actively 'Seeking' objects to your right and to your left sides, while also cognitively identifying particular objects to your right and to the left. Through cognitive seeking, your brain regains depth perception and in turn peripheral clarity. After your brain gains this vital data, it's internal GPS regains its signal. Essential your brain now knows where it is in relation to everything else.

If you're training for battle, its essential that you begin developing the habit of scanning your environment. Your brain is a muscle. The more you work a muscle, the fitter it becomes. By habitually keeping your head on a swivel, as you traverse the world around you, your brain develops an unconscious ability of being Situationally Aware. When it comes to Tactical Awareness, perfecting your 'After Action Scan' in training, helps your brain develop the unconscious ability to actively 'Seek' when your life is threatened. The more you perform this technique, the more ingrained it becomes.

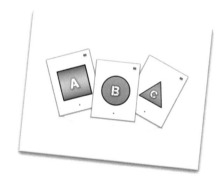

The best way to perfect the After Action Scan, is to incorporate ABCs Tactical Awareness Aides in your training. They are specifically designed to cause your eyes to see and your brain to process, multiple different objects while also performing instantaneous calculations, to train your brain to quickly differentiate one thing from another. To learn more about how ABCs Tactical Awareness Aides can make you more aware, turn to Page 134.

After Action Scan

The After Action Scan is a cognitive based search and destroy technique. It's not a meaningless and lazy side-to-side movement of one's head. Too often you will see that fatal error being performed on many a firearms range, as they simply move their heads absent any though whatsoever. Shooters have either forgotten or failed to be properly educated on the purpose of this life saving technique. The purpose is to 'Seek' and 'Find' additional Threats to one's safety. It is also to 'Seek' and 'Find' locations of available cover. Falling into the habit of simply moving your head left and right, without cognitively seeking, will encode the movement without the thought, leaving you incapable of being able to maintain Tactical Awareness during a fight.

1st Check Left

NOTE: Check Left. After Action Scan is vital to maintaining effective situational awareness. During direct contact with your Treat, your body will naturally cause your vision to focus on your Threat which such a degree of clarity that everything else around you fades out of view. Encoding proper After Action Scans will allow your brain to literally recalibrate and allow for you to regain normal visual function.

2nd Check Right

NOTE: Now check right. Don't get lazy in training! Remember you're teaching yourself to ACTIVELY look or seek for something. You're not simply moving your head. Scan and SEEK out possible Threats and or positions of possible cover. Remember to look back at your Threat each time you scan from left to right.

3rd Check Left & Behind

NOTE: Now it's time to look behind you. Start by looking over your left shoulder. Remember to cognitively identify an object while doing so in training. This trains your brain to instinctively SEEK as opposed to blindly gaze.

4th Check Right & Behind

NOTE: Now it's time to look over your right shoulder. As you transition right, be sure to identify your Threat to assure they're no-longer a threat. As you look over your right shoulder you should also cognitively identify an object behind you. Our ingenious ABCs Tactical Awareness Aides are the best way to perfect your After Action Scans. They're inexpensive and extremely easy to use.
Use them each time you train.

Engaging Multiple Threat:

Our bodies are designed in a way that we can only do <u>ONE</u> thing effectively at any given time. Forget about Hollywood action movies, where you see someone running from one place to another, engaging a mass of enemy fighters, all while blazing away with two guns. Arming yourself with two guns only makes you twice as useless. The answerer to defeating multiple Threats comes down to strategy. While your enemies play Checkers, you're going to play Tactical Chess. This is accomplished in two ways:

1. **Spreading the Love:** If you have multiple Threats actively engaging you, it means you need to actively engage them as simultaneously as possible. Shoot them all, equally. The more time you spend engaging one particular Threat, means your other Threat(s) have more time to engage you.

    - One way to Spread the Love, is to shoot in a pattern. If you have (2) Threats, you would shoot each Threat once or twice, then quickly transition and shoot the other once or twice.

    - Another way is to randomly engage each Threat. Maybe you have (3) Threats and you choose to shoot your closest Threat three times, your next Threat twice and your last Threat once. Then you shoot your closest Threat once, move next Threat and shoot them twice and end by shooting your last Threat in the head.

2. **Movement:** By moving you make yourself a much harder target to kill. Also through the action of movement, you begin the process of causing your Threats to react to you.

    - One way is to use a blocking technique. This is accomplished by moving at angles so as to place objects, blind spots or even your Threat's accomplices, between you and your closest Threat. The idea is to eliminate a particular Threat's ability to continue engaging you, because they either can't see you or you've placed an object between them making it harder to engage you.

    - Another technique is to increase distance between you and your Threats. By increasing the distance, you decrease the amount of hip rotation and torso movement required to "Spread The Love." This is because as you move back and away from your Threats, you gain an ever increasing view of them. Pretty soon they will all be in front of you, making them much easier engage.

    - Flanking your Threats is another example of this. As opposed to moving backwards, you simply rush to the far right or left side of one of your Threats. At some point during this movement you will essentially have all of your Threat's lined up like ducks in a row. You will also create a situation where your farthest Threats have to shoot through or past their buddies in order to engage you. That's what's called a 'Force Multiplier' in the tactical world.

However, you choose to engage multiple Threats, you need to do so dynamically, with speed and with violence of action. You need to turn the tables as quickly as possible, and cause your Threats to react to you. The wolves who seek your blood may have trained to coordinate their attacks; it is however very unlikely they've trained in coordinating a response to your attack. Turn the tide, be quick and be deadly.

12
Defensive Shooting

The Laws of Combat and their effect on the human body, creates a substantial conundrum of sorts, when it relates to marksmanship. Hits count! On the range it can mean the difference between a pat on the back or a trophy at your next 3 Gun match. In a fight for your life though, a miss could mean you don't go back to your family. The problem is that most shooters build their entire defensive shooting posture, on sand. When the Apocalyptic Tsunami of Combat comes, its affect washes away one's ability to remain accurate. This is precisely why police officers have a pitiful 20% hit ratio in real-world shootouts. Their attackers have a 90% hit ration. Why, because when you're under attack, your 'Reacting' to a completely unknown Threat to your existence.

The concept of 'Marksmanship' is not easily translated in a tactical environment. With that being said, there is a huge difference between 'Range Marksmanship' and 'Tactical Marksmanship'.

Marksmanship on the range is accomplished by mastering eight important elements. The level of one's expertise, is depended upon their ability to effectively balance all eight components, in a harmonious orchestra of kinesis.

1. Stance
2. Grip
3. Sight Alignment
4. Sight Picture
5. Breathing
6. Trigger Control
7. Follow Through
8. Trigger Reset

On the Range; where there is a complete absence of Combat Stress, these (8) components to accuracy, are the ingredients to a bull's-eye. On the range you have the ability to think through, slowdown and control each movement independently. However, in a gunfight your ability to control your movements, is greatly diminished. In a gunfight, you're franticly reacting to a lethal Threat, you're not shooting bulls-eyes. As discussed previously, the Laws of Combat and their overall effect on your physiology to a great extent, prevent you from achieving the (2) most important elements of 'Range Marksmanship' while also greatly diminishing (4) others. This means in a gunfight your left with the possibility of only being effective in but (2) areas of Marksmanship.

A Two Legged Stool:

Have you ever attempted to sit on a two legged stool? It can be done, but it requires a constant awareness of balance and an absence of distraction. What do you think the overall affect (10) shots of rum would have, on your ability to control your balance, while attempting to sit on a stool with only two legs? The intoxicating effects from the cocktail of Combat is unmatched. If you rely on Range Marksmanship in a gunfight, you're gonna miss 80% of the time. Here's why:

1. **Non-existent Sights:** Sight use is the cornerstone to effective marksmanship at the range. Force Science has proven that it is virtually impossible to even see your gun-sights in a gunfight. The physiology of a gunfight, means the only thing you'll see; with clarity, is the person(s) trying to kill you. This all important Law of Combat, is as catastrophic as a nuclear meltdown if your gun-fighting skills have been built on the tenets of Traditional Sight Use, or Sight Alignment and Sight Picture.

2. **Soup Sandwich:** The very same Laws of Combat greatly hamper our ability to perform (4) more all important elements to success on the range.

    - Your ability to control breathing is non-existent. You will breath but it will be fast and it will be random. The idea of shooting at the end of your exhale in close Combat, is impossible.
    - Trigger manipulation is also diminished. This represents (3) equally important functions:
        - Trigger Control
        - Follow-Through
        - Trigger Reset.

The reality is that in combat; unless you've undergone Procedural Memory training; like ZuluFight, you're going to slap, yank and jerk your trigger. What you're left with is a Soup Sandwich that tastes a lot like the stuff that comes out of a cow's ass. Losing your ability to hit your Threat, while they effortlessly put holes in you, is a pitifully bitter pill to swallow.

Combat Hydraulics:

As discussed previously, Combat is the most chaotically charged, out of control, consistently dynamic environment one will ever find themselves. It's measured in splits of seconds and its force is greater than the convergence of entire oceans. The only way to assure you react with a Tactical Squared Response, is by preparing for that battled beforehand. This is accomplished in (3) ways:

1. **Training The Psyche:** The first ingredient to s Tactical Squared Response is by preparing your mind for the psychology of Combat. It's vital that you devour and understand the science of Combat itself. You must learn about its effects and how you can counter or better manage them. Having a firm grasp on this all-important truth, will prevent you from experiencing 'Combat Paralysis' or Condition Black as Col. Cooper put it. Knowing what WILL happen physiologically, will greatly decrease the psychological effects. Preparing today, will assuring you choose a training method, which will actually translate to a 'Win' tomorrow.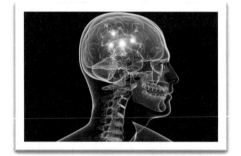

2. **Training The Body:** The next step is to adopt and commit yourself to a practical training system capable of encoding the appropriate Fight Responses, for tomorrow's battle. Sun Tzu tells us that a skilled warrior fights his battle a thousand times before he's even met his enemy. Training your body; by developing the habits of success, is a vital ingredient to success in Combat. The ZuluFight Dry-Fire Training System is the easiest way at achieve this. There is no better way to prepare one's body for war and to master the Kata of Firearms Self-Defense, than through Procedural Memory Encoding. It's how the Samurai of old became so deadly and its exactly how the members of our Special Operations Community train for battle. Mastering the kinesis of battle, requires a copious amount of repetition over an extended period of time. There's no better way to do this than through Dry-Fire Training. ZuluFight takes Dry-Fire to a whole new level of mastery. It's how you'll develop practical, effective and deadly instinctive solutions for tomorrow's battle. Turn to Page 131 to learn more.

3. **Playing Tactical Chess:** The last ingredient to a Tactical Squared Response is the development of effective Fighting Tactics. In a gunfight, your voodoo needs to be better than your Threat's. What you do in response to their attack, WILL determine all. We all know that book-smart geek; the know-it-all, who couldn't find their way out of a Cracker Jacks box. Simply being book-smart and knowing the science behind Combat, is useless if you neglect to develop actual Fighting Skills based on that knowledge. Skills without strategy are meaningless in Combat. We've all likely met the guy who knows how to shoot a basketball and consistently make half-court shots, yet hasn't a clue on how to actually 'Play' a real game. The concept of 'Tactical Chess' is where you infuse proven, practical and effective Fighting Tactics into your Tactical Response. Movement, repetitive fire, cover and blocking techniques, these are all ingredients; that when melded together and directed in a controlled manner,

afford you the ability to place your Threat in checkmate and win the day. An easy and effective way to learn practical and proven battle techniques, is by attending tactical shooting classes. Seek out training classes that teach dynamic movement and Force-on-Force simulation. Zulu Tactical provides a number of tactical courses, focused on providing its students with tactical solutions that actually work. Seeking out competent instruction is how you turn knowledge into Combat effective action.

Tactical Shooting Positions:

Being able to shoot on the move and from a myriad of different positions, is a key ingredient to winning a gunfight. A true tactical shooting position means that once acquired, the shooter can effectively engage their Threat(s) accurately and constantly, without having to constantly change their base. The following are a few practical shooting positions which should be practiced and encoded:

Tactical Stance

NOTE: Your Tactical Stance is a vital ingredient to your overall fighting solution. The best most practical position should consist of a staggered stance with a comfortable bend in your knees. You should easily be able to move in any direction while also being able to absorb physical contact from any direction. This position should NOT change during the draw or while shooting and is the basis for a Modified Isosceles Stance.

Natural Shooting Stance

NOTE: Bring sights up and level to eyes not eyes to sights. Feet should be staggered with comfortable bend in knees. The Modified Isosceles Stance is hands down the BEST tactical stance. It allows for the best overall mobility. Notice firearms is level with eyes and focus is on threat NOT sights.

C. Q. B. Ready

NOTE: This position is a perfect shooting platform at close quarters but is also the natural position to obtain a two-handed grip. Your elbows are brought tight against your sides and your firearm placed directly in front of you and level. From this position your torso becomes a turret mounted gun. You aim by simply squaring your shoulders towards your Threat. The key to maintaining a level firearm from this position is to lock your wrists and positioning your elbows against your sides as opposed to resting them on your stomach.

SUL Ready

NOTE: SUL is Portuguese for 'South' the direction of the muzzle. Obtaining this grip is easily performed by indexing both thumbs together remembering the firearm always rests on top of your support hand. SUL is the most practical handgun carry position as it provides the safest muzzle disciple while also allowing for ease of draw. SUL is also the safest handgun carry position while moving and or maneuvering around obstacles. Drawing from SUL is easy. Simply pivot your thumbs while lifting and pushing your handgun up and out. As you extend your arms, allow your support hand to naturally pivot into your two-handed grip.

Close Ready

NOTE: Close Ready is intended for firing from contact distance or within two feet. Simply lock your gun arm tight against your side with an OVERGRIP of the handgun. Accurate shot placement is similar to C.Q.B. Ready. Utilize your torso and squared shoulders as a sort of turret aiming device. It's important to raise your support hand in front of you. It's inevitable that at this distance you will make physical contact with the Threat. Having your support arm positioned in this manner will help provide a solid defensive posture while also giving you the ability to maintain safe distance so your firearm can properly function and reload. Making contact on your Threat with the muzzle while shooting will turn your semi-auto handgun into a single-shot paperweight.

Warrior Mentality:

There is a difference between a 'Warrior' and a 'Fighter'. Above all else, your greatest chance of surviving a deadly encounter, rests on your internal obsession to 'Win' no matter the cost.

A Fighter, fights from a mindset rooted in competition. His goal is to beat his adversary by points and averages, while also accepting the belief that if his opponent is better, than a 'Lose' is probable. When it gets tough, when the sting of battle overwhelms him, the Fighter will concede for fear of injury.

To the contrary, the Warrior, fights with the mindset of a ruthless killer. To a certain degree, he's acquired a particular kind of bloodlust. He forgoes attempts of trying to avoid the unavoidable pain that's coming because he knows pain will come. Instead, his strategy is based on his expectation and acceptance of the sting of battle. He welcomes it with open arms because he has prepared for it ahead of time. He's developed a certain inoculation to pain and is ready to absorb its bite. He knows he will be shot, he will lose blood, he will experience injury, he will be caught off-guard, he will have to fight an uphill battle against all odds and that nothing will be fare. Yet he has already determined to kill his enemy, win the battle and return home.

While the Fighter fights to counter and avoid the inevitable, the Warrior has prepared and developed a solution capable of overcoming those odds, even under the worst conditions. Combat is not a competition, but basketball is and so are IPSC and 3 Gun matches. Combat is not a game; 'Call of Duty' is a game. Pin Pong, tennis, baseball, Risk.....These are competitions. Wrestling, MMA and UFC... these are extreme forms of competition. In a competition there are rules, parameters and limits. Both parties walk away to fight another day. In Combat there are no rules, no boundaries and no restraint. There are no second place Combat ribbons; those have been replaced with an obituary and a flag draped coffin. Failure in competition results in a loose, with a chance to meet again. Failure in Combat results in death, for which there is no coming back.

A competitor 'Stops' his opponent by countering their movements, thereby halting momentum. At some point their opponent concedes due to exhaustion or fear of injury. A Warrior on the other hand, stuns his enemy. He digs to his depths and retrieves the most instinctively vicious, most barbarically unrelenting and unimaginable carnage. His response completely surprises his Threat and sends shivers up their spine. The Warrior's fight is a brutally heinous, focused energy that jolts his antagonist at their core. It saps them of their willingness to proceed. At some point a Warrior's enemy actually believes they're looking into the eyes of a demonic being. That is the mentality of Warrior and the mindset you must acquire. You must devourer your enemy like a crazed lion.

FBI Miami Shootout April 11th 1986

- The gunfight lasted just over 4-minutes.
- Both suspects were shot within the first 30-seconds.
- The first suspect; Matix, sustained multiple gunshot wounds and injured multiple officers. Matix continued to fight for over 3-minutes before finally dying.
- The second suspect, Platt's first wound was the fatal shot. His first wound was from a 9mm through his right shoulder. It entered his chest, collapsed a lung and penetrated his heart.
- Platt continued to fight and killed with ease for 3 ½ more minutes.
- Platt advanced on Agents killing two and severely injuring five more Agents.
- Platt sustained eleven more wounds while advancing on Agents. Eight of those wounds were to the chest.
- Platt used three firearms. His own, Matix's and even executed his own killer with that Agent's own weapon before, dying 2 ½ minutes later. How's that for irony?
- Platt's cause of death was his first wound. By the end of the shooting he had 1 ½ liters of blood in his longs and died by drowning.
- When interviewed, the final Agent left standing informed investigators that there was a turning-point in the battle, where that Agent made the conscious

decision to actually 'Kill' Platt not just 'Stop' him. He expressed that it wasn't until he determined to 'Kill' his attacker, that the tides changed.

Florida Highway Shooting

- A suspect attempts to disarm a trooper during a traffic stop.
- Trooper shoots the suspect once in the upper abdomen with a contact shot from his 1911 45 ACP service pistol, but chooses not to keep shooting.
- Suspect retrieves his concealed Derringer .22 caliber. Then shoots and kills the trooper with one shot in the trooper's armpit.

Utah Mall Active Shooter

- Shootout occurred at a distance of 4-feet, between SWAT and the suspect.
- SWAT shot the suspect with nine fatal shots in the chest from full-auto MP5s. The suspect's heart exploded as the result of the first two of these rounds.
- The suspect continued to fight and shot at the SWAT Operators with a shotgun, barely missing one of the Operator's heads.
- The suspect was finally killed with six more full-auto shots to his head.

Oregon Suicidal Subject

- A suicidal female advances on 2 Deputies from 60-meters, while shooting at them with her Glock 17.
- The Deputies' 1st shot was fatal. He literally blew the suspect's heart open with a 1oz shotgun slug.
- Suspect continued to advance while shooting without staggering.
- Suspect closes to within 20-yards sustaining three more wounds.
- Suspect collapsed to the ground due to blood lose, but was still able to fire at the Deputies.
- Suspect turned the gun on herself, shot herself three times in the chest and two times in the face.
- Cause of death was ruled to be the final shot to the face.
- Another example that just because you inflict a 'Fatal' shot to your Threat, even if it blows their heart open, it doesn't mean the fight is over. You have to 'Kill' them before they die.

These are but a few examples of what actually occurs in gunfights. Sadly, the list could go on and on. None of these individuals were intoxicated or high on drugs at the time of the incidents. All of them were determined to kill the good guys. All of them sustained devastating and fatal wounds at the onset of the battle. All of them continued to fight regardless of their wounds. Just because your Threat's heart is blow apart, it does NOT mean you won. Science says they could still fight for up to four more minutes.

In a real gunfight, victory goes to he who's more determined to 'Kill'. Platt is a perfect example of this. Agent Ben Gorgan blew Platt's heart open with his first round. Yet Platt was more determined. Platt became the hunter. Platt advanced while laying down fire with his Mini-14, pinning down Agent Gorgan. Platt was hit numerous times during that advance, yet he still tracked Agent Gorgan down and shot him execution style. At that point in the battle, it was eight to one with the odds stacked against Platt. Platt took six of them out of the fight single handed.

The FBI's excuse for such an unbelievable ass kicking was ammunition. For the last 30-years the FBI has staunchly blamed their failure that day on the 9mm Luger, claiming it to be an inferior round in battle. They went as far as to develop the 40 S&W, which has proved to be a pathetically poor substitute. Finally, after all this time they have accepted the truth and have returned to the 9mm Luger as their go to round. Why, because they knew all along that their failure that day was because they failed to properly train their Agents for war.

It wasn't the rounds fired which proved to be ineffective, it was the inferiority of the Agents' fight. It was a defeated mindset which was founded on inaccurate assumptions of Combat, that caused Agents to accept defeat itself. It was their inferior training, which lacked the strategy. It was the Agent's inability to employ solid Team Tactics, so as to coordinate their response, which caused them to be pinned down and overrun. The suspects however, had the mindsets of ravage lions. They knew what to expect before they got there. Most notably, they were NOT going to stop killing until their bodies were drained of its blood. They acceded pain and welcomed its sting. They knew what mattered most was the speed, the veracity and the violence of their action. They knew the faster they were able to inflict multiple hits on their pursuers, the quicker they'd fall. They were trained to take the fight to the enemy and 'Kill' with vengeance.

Your survival in a gunfight is completely depended upon your will to 'Kill' your Threat, before they kill you. Your ability to kill your Threat is completely depended upon your degree of preparation. Your preparation is measured by your knowledge of the dynamics of Combat, your aptitude with your weapon and your overall ability to turn the tide of the battle, through the application of solid fighting tactics.

It's about the 'Violence of Action' not mere action. When you violently send rapidly expanding rounds into multiple different areas of your Threat's body, it initiates total body meltdown. As those rounds impact, electric currents are sent through their

Central Nervous System like ripples on calm water. However, by sending multiple rounds in close succession, those ripples intersect, thereby scrambling the pattern and completely disrupting their brains ability to decipher what's happing. Meltdown begins, their blood becomes thin and unable to clot. Their blood pressure and heart rate skyrockets, bringing about a catastrophic failure as their blood pours from wound to wound.

When you face your Threat you must NOT mistake that he is trying to kill you. Unless you kill them first, he WILL achieve his objective. There are no do-overs, no time-outs and no re-spawning. In Combat, defeat is fatal and it is final. It's up to you to determine today that you will win, no matter the cost.

Practical Exercises

The trainee will be given opportunity to gain practical proficiency in Handgun Safety, Basic Operation and its Tactical use, through the performance of the following exercise. These exercise will be performed with both Dry and Hot. The trainee will show these proficiencies through the use of both their personal firearm as well as specialized training simulation handguns. The trainee MUST prove they are proficient in the basic operation of their firearm, as well as show proficiency in the following Defensive Shooting exercise, in order to receive Zulu Tactical certification for this class.

ZuluSafe Cardinal Safety Rules:

The trainee will recite all four ZuluSafe Cardinal Safety Rules, to demonstrate its retention and will show proficiency in its retention; through its adherence, throughout each practical exercise.

1. Treat ALL firearms as if they are ALWAYS loaded.
2. Keep your fingers OFF the trigger and OUTSIDE the trigger-guard until you are justified and ready to shoot.
3. NEVER point your muzzle at anything or anyone you're not justified and willing to kill.
4. Be SURE of your Threat and what stands beyond.

Basic Operation:

The trainee will be instructed in and will show proficiency in the following procedures. Snap-Caps / Dummy Rounds will be used to simulate loading, unloading and malfunctions.

Clearing:

1. Point your muzzle in a safe direction assuring your finger stays off the trigger and outside the trigger guard.
2. Remove and stow the magazine from the magwell.
3. Lock the Slide back using the Slide Lock mechanism. (if not equipped w/Slide Lock, hold slide open)

4. Visually & manually (i.e. w/support hand pinky) inspect the magwell to assure there is no magazine and therefore nothing to FEED your handgun.

5. Visually & manually (i.e. w/support hand pinky) inspect the breach & chamber to assure there is no ammunition present and therefore nothing for your handgun to EAT.

6. Repeat steps 4&5 for a total of 3 times to make sure your handgun is completely empty and 'Clear' of any ammunition.

7. Return Slide to battery by releasing the slide-lock mechanism or racking the slide itself.

Component Manipulation:

The trainee will be instructed in and will show proficiency in the unique components & functions of their training handgun i.e. safeties, trigger, locks, de-cocks etc.

Loading & Unloading:

The trainee will be instructed in and will show proficiency in the performance of safe loading and unloading procedures with their provided training firearm, to include it's magazine, through the use of Snap-Caps.

Basic Marksmanship:

The trainee will be instructed in and will show proficiency in the following procedures.

1. Stance
2. Grip
3. Sight Alignment
4. Sight Picture
5. Breathing
6. Trigger Control
7. Follow Through
8. Trigger Reset

After Action Scan:

The trainee will be instructed in and will show proficiency in appropriate After Action Scans through the use of ABCs Tactical Awareness Aides.

DELTA Threat ID:

The trainee will be instructed in and will show proficiency in the retention of the five step DELTA Threat ID process, by describing each step and what they are 'Looking' for.

1. Whole Body
2. Hands
3. Waist
4. Arm span
5. Demeanor

ZuluFight Sight Picture:

Using the 'Point' method, the trainee will identify the Threat Picture on the wall in front of them and will do the following:

1. Focus on the Threat's nose.
2. Extend and point at the Threat's nose with their strong hand.
3. While still focusing on the Threat, they will gain peripheral awareness of their extended index finger; which should appear fussy, as it's pointing at the Threat's nose. This is a ZuluFight Sight Picture.
4. Trainee will now shift focus to their index finger.
5. While still focusing on their index finger, trainee will gain peripheral awareness of the Threat's face, which should appear fussy. Trainee will notice the Threat's features are indiscernible even at such a close range. This is Traditional Sight Picture.

ZuluFight Simulation:

The trainee will be instructed in and will show proficiency in the following procedures.

1. CQB Ready Position
2. Sul Ready Position
3. Holstered Position
4. Combat Reload
5. Tactical Reload
6. Type 1 Malfunction
7. Type 2 Malfunction
8. Type 3 Malfunction

Defensive Shooting:

The trainee will be instructed in multiple Defensive Shooting exercises. They will be shown the higher tempo reality of this type of shooting vs. that of basic firearms marksmanship. The training must show proficiency and an ability to maintain appropriate safety as stress is increased, in order to advance and receive certification.

Multi-Threat Engagements:

The trainee will be instructed on ways to overcome multiple attacking Threats. They will be given opportunity to engage both near and far threats at varying angles.

Force on Force:

The trainee will participate in multiple forms of Force on Force scenarios. This will consist of both low stress walkthroughs as well as high stress, high tempo engagements. Scenarios will be tailored to test the trainees overall Defensive Firearms effectiveness.

Whether you're a civilian or armed professional, this breakthrough system will take your firearms proficiency to an unthinkable level. With an exponential increase in random violent crime, deadly confrontations have become a new norm in nearly every community, from urban centers to the countryside.

Firearms Self-Defense is much for than accuracy on a range or high scores in competition. Face-to-face confrontations are the most fluidly dynamic environment you'll ever encounter. The realities and consequences associated with gunfights, often come at the highest costs. Sadly, the vast majority of training techniques are dangerous and useless at best, especially when attempted in real-life gunfights. Adding fuel to the fire, most so called 'Firearms Experts' endorse fatally impractical tactics, which attempt to defy the scientific realities of conflict itself.

ZuluFight is founded on the irrefutable physical parameters associated with deadly encounters. It utilizes the most scientifically recognized method of firearms training; Dry-Fire, enabling you an ability to encode perfect movement. But not all Dry-Fire methods are equal. The vast majority focus too heavily on only two aspects of shooting, the draw and trigger squeeze. ZuluFight masters the kinesis of shooting, turning Dry-Fire into a Kata. This allows you the capability of honing every single aspect of shooting. In fact, ZuluFight is a 'Total Training System' in that you're able to isolate and master each ingredient to a sound Fight Response, everything from:

- Start Positions, Stance, Presentation & Trigger Manipulation
- Reloads & Malfunction Mitigation
- Holsters & Slings
- After Action Tactical Awareness & Fight Psychology
- As well as all eight firearms fundamentals

Best of all, ZuluFight is specifically designed for handguns, rifles and even shotguns. It's cookbook format is straightforward and easy to follow. There's no re-occurring cost, no ammunition, no trips to the range and is achieved from the comforts of your own home.

The advantages of this lifesaving system, is your key to tomorrow's victory. ZuluFight will boost your accuracy more than any other method. You'll gain real proficiency, while exponentially decreasing response time, for an instantaneous kinesthetic response. Discover the secret of winning tomorrow's battle today. Train today so you're ready tomorrow!

Don't Hesitate. Perfect your Kata TODAY!

zulutactical.com/zulufight

Are you prepared for the all-encompassing legal battle you'll face, when you use Deadly Force? The most overlooked aspect of Self-Defense has to do with what comes after the incident.

The complicated and completely unavoidable obstacles, which immediately follow every use of Deadly Force, requires a very unique and preemptive strategy, if one hopes to come out unscathed. Sadly, most civilians and attorneys alike, save the planning for tomorrow. A sad reality is you can be completely justified, cleared of all Criminal wrongdoing and still be found liable in a Civilly proceeding. Meaning, it's completely possible to be stuck paying millions, for doing the right thing.

However, there are important, practical steps you can take today, to avoid tomorrow's legal onslaught. This step-by-step system is your preemptive approach, for an impenetrable legal defense. ZuluShield is a must have for anyone who may one day be forced to protect life with a firearm or even with their hands. Whether you're a private citizen or a seasoned police officer, ZuluShield is your solution to the most complicated legal problems.

Learn what you can do today and the vitally important things you must do directly following such an incident, to avoid a legal catastrophe. Get protected today, discover the secrets for a bulletproof Firearms Legal Defense. Prepare today so you're ready tomorrow!

Don't Hesitate. Get Protected TODAY!

zulutactical.com/zulushield

 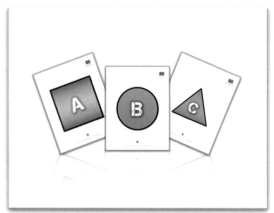

- Stay Aware & Stay Alive -

When it comes to deadly confrontations, one constant remains true, there is always a significant risk of like. Your survival is dependent upon your ability to remain Tactically Aware, even under the most extreme stress. It comes down to how well you're able to calculate the totality of the circumstances presented and employ a solution that's based on strategy. It's a calculative response, rather than one that's purely reactive by nature.

What are ABCs Tactical Awareness Aides?

ABCs Tactical Awareness Aides are scientifically based training aides, capable of actually conditioning a high state of Cognitive Awareness in high stress, fluid environments. ABCs placards are specifically designed to condition your brain's ability to multi-task with clarity, even under the most extreme levels of stress. ABCs are easy to use and can be included in almost any training environment, for a multitude of functions.

ABCs Tactical Awareness Aides packages include:

- Highly visible
- Durable & waterproof
- Easily fastened or held
- 9 full-color laminated placards
- 18 combinations of colors, shapes & letters

Here's how they work:

Situational Awareness is the Cognitive Association with one's environment. However, Tactical Awareness the ability to remain Situationally Aware, during times of extreme stress, such as deadly confrontations.

The dilemma, is that Tactical Awareness is a state-of-mind. It's not a tangible skillset like shooting, making it a difficult thing to master. It's a process of continually identifying and relating with your environment, with a very high degree of cognition. However, science tells us cognitive function exponentially diminishes as stress levels increase. So developing a habit of Tactical Awareness, requires a very unique scientific approach, that's achieved through repetition.

ABCs Tactical Awareness Aides are an ingenious and simple way to achieve this, because they use kindergarten level brain development techniques, as a means of giving your brain an ability to 'Think' under stress.

When it comes to Firearms Self-Defense, one of the most widely practiced techniques and an attempt at conditioning Tactical Awareness, is the 'After Action Scan.' Basically, the shooter scans their environment; left and right, after the course of fire, so as to seek for possible hazards and threats or places of potential cover. However, what's missing on nearly every range is the 'Seeking' element. Most After Action Scans become a mere physical turn of one's head, a glance and a look. In order to actually 'Seek', you've gotta have something to seek, as well as a particular level of Active Thought. You need to actually see something and identify it, thereby giving it a value in relation to other objects in its environment.

To correctly condition Tactical Awareness, you have to go about including repetitively Cognitive Association drills in training, which activate four important brain functions:

- Visual
- Associative
- Intellectual
- Verbal

Including ABCs placards in your training regime, makes this a simple process. In Kindergarten our vocabulary was founded on the building blocks of the ABCs. Likewise, ABCs placards, give you an ability to sustain Cognitive Association, by conditioning your brain to continually identify and associate,

- Color
- Shape
- Name

While this may appear elementary, be assured, the task becomes difficult when combining it with some type of kinesthetic function like shooting i.e. After Action Scan. What it does is force the brain to multi-task,

- Visually (see the object)
- Associatively (identify its composition)
- Intellectually (associate & differentiate its qualities)
- Verbally (communicate its value)

Each time the user identifies and values an ABCs placard, they've completed a very important back-and-forth conversation of sorts, with the left and right hemispheres of the brain. Overtime, the task becomes easier, thereby honing the user's comprehensive decision making through Active Thought.

How can ABCs Tactical Awareness Aides be used?

ABC's are extremely multi-faceted and can be used in a number of different training environments. The idea is to condition practical and fluid awareness. So, for skills which require divided attention ABCs will take that ability to a whole new level.

Firearms Self-Defense:

ABCs placards can be used to aide with After Action Scans or even placed on or near targets to assist in training Threat ID & Association.

Reconnaissance & Surveillance Training:

ABCs placards can be positioned in various places in the training environment to help gage and test a trainee's level of awareness and attention to detail.

Tactical Operations Training:

ABCs placards can be positioned throughout a building during entry drills, forcing members of the Entry element to visual and verbally identify ABC's as they pass through the structure, forcing them to multi-task at speed and under stress.

Emergency Vehicle Operation Training:

Anyone who's worked as a First Responder, knows the stress and dynamics of simply driving to the scene. ABC's placards can take EVOC to a whole new level and help condition a trainee to multi-task visually and verbally while also completing the other multitude of functions while driving.

Those are just a few of the many ways ABCs Tactical Awareness Aides can be used. How you'll use them depends on your imagination. Think outside the box and make your training the best training possible. Take your training to the next level. Gaining Tactical Awareness is as easy as the ABCs.

Don't Hesitate. Stay Aware TODAY!

zulutactical.com/abcs

ZuluWarrior Training Group:

Are you ready to experience the most repeatable, realistic and reliable firearms training program giving you the most practical solution for tomorrow's deadly encounter? Are you ready to learn realistic tactics so you can play Tactical Chess while your threat plays Checkers? Use the QR Code to the right or visit our website today!

zulutactical.com/training

TeamZulu:

Stay up to date with all things *ZULU*. Connect with us on Facebook. Learn why fans from around the World choose *ZULU*. Use the QR Code to the right or visit our website today!

facebook.com/zulutac

Notes

Disclaimer

ZULU TACTICAL LLC its members and associates assume no responsibility or liability whatsoever for the use of this firearms training manual or participation in the Intro Handgun Defense (IHD) firearms training course. The objective of the IHD course and this firearms training manual is to introduce the trainee and user to the realities of firearms self-defense and confrontation so as to provide said trainee and user with an assortment of practical, effective and safe ways to survive such a mortally dangerous encounter. Firearms safety is vitally important and is the sole responsibility and liability of the trainee and user. It is the sole responsibility and liability of the trainee and user to know the status of their firearm at all times and to treat their firearm as though it is always loaded, all the time. It is the sole responsibility and liability of the trainee and user to follow all four ZuluSafe Cardinal Firearms Rules at all times to assure the use of their firearm is safe, responsible and prudent. The trainee and user understand that any and all firearms training and use is inherently dangerous and has the potential to cause serious physical injury and or death. There is also an increased risk of lead exposure and hearing loss associated with firearms training and use. By participating in the IHD course and by using this firearms training manual, the trainee and user assumes sole responsibility and liability. ZULU TACTICAL LLC, its members and associates make no guarantees or promises concerning the use of this information and tactics associated with this course and manual. The trainee and user understand that firearms confrontation and self-defense is among the most dangerously fluid and unpredictable circumstance one could ever find themselves in. Although skills gained from this firearms training course and manual can be effective in surviving an armed attack, there are no guarantees to surviving such an encounter. When it relates to firearms and self-defense tactics, the intent of this course and manual is to communicate practical and effective ways of overcoming attack. The tactics, principles and understandings communicated in the course and manual are intended to be considered as options. If any part of this course and manual is adopted by the trainee or user, the trainee and user assumes full sole responsibility and liability of the use of these tactics. Furthermore, ZULU TACTICAL LLC its members and associates encourages the trainee and user to seek further professional firearms training from a variety of certified firearms experts so as to have as broad and balanced an understanding of this topic as possible. ZULU TACTICAL LLC, its members and associates are not attorneys and do not dispense legal advice. The information contained in this course and its manual should NOT be construed as legal advice. This information is intended to provide the trainee and user broad general guidelines regarding the legal use of firearms and self-defense. For more specific information, it is the sole responsibility and liability of the trainee and user to seek out and consult an attorney familiar with the laws relating to firearms use, self-defense and the use of deadly force. It is the sole responsibility and liability of the trainee and user to consult an attorney and become familiar with local, state and federal laws related to firearms possession and ownership, firearms use for training and self-defense and the use of deadly force to assure that future use and possession is protected and within the guidelines of local, state and federal laws.

INTRO HANDGUN DEFENSE Copyright © 2014 Zulu Tactical L.L.C. All rights reserved. No part of this document, system or course may be reproduced or transmitted in any form or by any means, electronic or mechanical, including photocopy, recording, or any other information storage and retrieval system, without the written permission of Zulu Tactical LLC.

Made in the USA
Columbia, SC
19 September 2024